Adventures of Kado

By
Alice Mertie Underhill

TEACH Services, Inc.
PUBLISHING
www.TEACHServices.com

Copyright © 1953 Pacific Press Publishing Association
Copyright © 2005 TEACH Services, Inc.
ISBN-13: 978-1-57258-368-9
Library of Congress Control Number: 2005932289

Published by

TEACH Services, Inc.
P U B L I S H I N G
www.TEACHServices.com

PREFACE

The story of Kado is lovingly dedicated to my sister who, with her husband, a physician, spent many years in the land of the Telugus, in Ganjam District, India.

As a missionary she has many stories to tell of her life and experiences in faraway India, where, side by side with her husband, she cared for the sick in the hospital, taught in the mission school, and helped to break the hold of superstition and the worship of idols and devil gods among the Telugus.

May these stories of Kado inspire many boys and girls to share their faith. May they learn to trust completely in the God in heaven, and await the return of their Friend and Saviour, Jesus Christ.

—THE AUTHOR.

The mother looked at her sleeping son as he lay on his little mat.
He was a strong little boy, but the mother remembered evil
spirits were near.

LET'S MEET KADO

ON HIS small mat on the hard mud floor of a rude hut in faraway India, lay a tiny brown baby boy, fast asleep. His mother beside him had just awakened, for the first rays of the morning sun were coming into the open doorway, shining down from over the tall trees of the jungle. His father was out in the yard behind the house, milking the cow. There would be warm, rich milk to go with the rice for breakfast.

Before arising to prepare the rice, the mother turned to look at her sleeping son. He looked so tiny and innocent as he lay on his wee mat. How wonderful it was to have a little son in the home. He was a lovely baby. But, oh! she must not speak her thoughts aloud, for fear the spirits would hear her and take her baby away from her. Very soon his father must take a generous gift to the charm doctor. Only then would they feel that no evil would come to their home. The mother gently touched the little brown bare feet. Then she arose to prepare breakfast of rice for herself and her husband.

Upon three small stones in the corner of the room sat a smoky black kettle of rice. She built a fire between the stones, and soon the breakfast was ready. When the milking was done, the man of the family came in, ready to eat. Seated on the floor, with the bowl of steaming rice between them, they lifted out the rice with their hands, placing it upon large leaves, from which they ate it with their fingers.

"Have you thought of a name for our son?" asked the father, proudly looking at his sleeping baby.

The mother shook her head. "I have not decided," she said.

"I have thought of many names," continued the father; "but we must be careful. If we should call him by a nice name, the spirits will think he is of great value, and they will take him from us. Perhaps we should call him 'Red Onions,' or 'Bad Luck,' or 'Dirty Water.'"

"I think we shall call him 'Kado,'" said mother tenderly. "It is different, and our son, too, will be different. Someday he will be big and strong like his father."

"And kind and good like his mother," added the father with a smile.

"I want him to learn many things that will help make him wise and useful. Yes, our little Kado will be different," said mother.

Day by day his parents could notice that Kado was growing big and strong. He smiled. He made queer sounds in his throat as though he were trying to speak. One day he discovered his own brown toes. How he laughed in glee as they wiggled up and down on his mat.

Soon Kado was creeping all over the room. But mother was always on guard to keep her little son from harm. Kado must learn to stay back from the hot rice kettle upon the three hot smoky stones in the corner. He must not crawl outside the little doorway—not yet. First, he must learn that the outside world is full of dangers: snakes, bears, leopards, tigers, and other wild animals.

When mother went out into the bright sunshine, she took little Kado with her. He learned to ride on her back or hip, fastened securely within the folds of her sari, which was a wrap-around garment, her only necessary piece of clothing. Kado would ride to the spring, where mother filled an earthen jar with water and carried it upon her head or shoulder. They went many times each day to the spring, for mother could carry only one jar at a time.

Sometimes Kado would ride to the forest when mother went for wood. Mother took a little hatchet to chop off small branches. She would carry a large bundle of sticks on her head to be used at home for fuel to cook rice, lentils, curry, and beans. Kado enjoyed these days in the forest with mother. Many of the village women went in a group to gather their supply of wood. They felt more secure in case some wild animal should be lurking near. When Kado became tired, he just rested his little brown head against mother. He would sleep while mother went about her task of gathering wood.

When the party returned home, Kado was glad to have his share of rice and curry that mother prepared in the black kettle that sat over the fire between the three stones in the corner.

Kado did not stay little. He grew and grew like any normal baby. Soon he was big enough to run about. He followed his father to the rice fields. He liked to help pick up roots when father plowed the fields. He helped gather stones to build the bund, the little mud-and-stone fence around the rice terrace. The bund kept the water in the field so the rice could grow.

Soon Kado was big enough to go with father to herd the cattle, and to take the big water buffaloes to the pond to be washed. The boy carried a little stick in his hand to help keep the cattle on the trail. The big water buffaloes looked fierce and dangerous with their long sweeping horns; but father was close beside Kado, and the boy knew they would not hurt him.

There were many things to fear—things that could be seen and things one could not see. There were bears, tigers, leopards, and snakes that could be seen; but Kado was also told that there were ghosts and spirits that could not be seen. These were mostly to be feared. You never could know just when they might accidentally stop under a spirit's tree. The spirits would become very angry and would cause harm to come to you. Then you must go to the charm doctor so that he could break the spell. When Kado grew older, he was also taught to fear Christians and missionaries. If you went near them or talked to them, they would cast a spell upon you and you would become a Christian. Then all manner of trouble would come to you and your family, but the charm doctor would be powerless to help you.

Kado was a happy boy. He was made even happier by the arrival of three little brothers, Tari, Lesso, and Con. As each little brown brother was added to the family, father made a special visit to the charm doctor, taking him a gift so that no evil would befall the new baby or the family,

Kado loved his younger brothers. They played with him by the pool, watching the older boys wash the huge water buffaloes to keep them cool. Often Kado would carry little Con upon his hip when he helped drive the cattle to the pond and back again to the enclosure behind the house for the night.

What fun it was, after a long, hard day of work in the rice paddies, to sit in a circle around the family rice bowl with father, mother, and his three brothers. When supper was over, they spread their garments upon the hard-packed dirt floor and went to sleep.

KADO AND THE MYNA

I T WAS early morning. Kado blinked when he openedhis eyes, for the sunbeams winked at him from above the tall jungle trees. He stretched himself, put on his wrap-around garment, and started to go to the spring for water. Just as he pushed open the door, a snake dropped from the thatched roof and fell to the ground at the boy's feet.

"Oh," cried Kado, "A snake, a snake!"

He jumped back in alarm, nearly upsetting little Con in his haste to get away from the snake. But the snake slid silently into the bushes and disappeared.

"Maybe that is a sign," whispered Tari, his brown eyes growing big in fear.

"Maybe our house is in the path of the spirits and they have sent the snake to warn us," suggested Lesso.

"Something terrible is sure to happen to us today," said Kado. "Perhaps we should not go to the forest to gather wood."

But mother assured the boys that all would be well. There would be many others gathering wood with them. "And," she added, "it is only natural for snakes to stretch out on the thatch above the door to catch the first warm rays of the morning sun. They like the sunshine, too."

So Kado filled his little gourd with rice and curry. Tari, Lesso, and Con also filled their gourds and hung them by fiber cords around their necks. This would be their noonday meal. Mother filled a larger gourd for father, who would be in the rice field all day. She also

As Kado opened the door, a snake dropped from the thatched roof and fell to the ground. The boy jumped back. "Maybe it's a sign," said Kado.

filled one for herself. Then the family were ready to start. Kado carried his hatchet to trim off the smaller branches. They waited at the end of the path for a group of women and children who also were going wood gathering.

Soon the group was ready to start up the trail to the forest. As they walked along they chatted merrily and exchanged bits of news of the village.

"Did you hear?" began one of the women. "One of my neighbors killed a huge python this morning. The man was out walking in the jungle, and he did not see the snake until it was too late to go back. He was so frightened that he prayed. You know, he has become a Christian. He prayed to his God, and then he shot the snake with an arrow. It was a big one, nine feet long, and weighed thirty pounds!"

"Well," said one of the women, nodding her head knowingly. "He must expect troubles to come to him, now that he has become a Christian. The charm doctor has warned him many times."

"He has been seen talking to the missionary," added another woman. "If the charm doctor learns of that, there is no telling what troubles and curses will come to him. But did you hear about my neighbor? He, too, has become a Christian. He also has been under the curse of the snakes. One day he was bitten by a snake, and his leg began to swell. Then he did what the missionary had told him to do. He prayed first, and then he took out his knife and cut the flesh where the bite was, and drew out the poison. He did not die."

Kado's mother listened. She was thinking of the snake that had fallen from the thatch roof that morning. She hoped that the curse of snakes had not come upon her. Kado also listened, and he was thinking. He said nothing, for sometimes it is better not to talk. The spirits might hear him if he spoke his thoughts aloud, and they would be angry. They might put the curse of snakes upon him, but why? He had not become a Christian; he had not talked to the missionary.

The group of wood gatherers arrived at a clearing in the forest, and each one began working in earnest. Kado did his part by cutting and chopping the smaller branches with his hatchet. But the day was very hot, and Kado grew tired. He placed his hatchet carefully within the folds of his garment and sat for a moment in the shade of a tree. He became quite drowsy and closed his eyes for a minute. Hearing a queer noise above his head, he opened his eyes and was instantly wide awake. Children of India must be always on the alert for danger. A snake? No, it was not a snake. It was only a bird on the branch above him, peering down at him with bright, beady eyes.

"Oh, a myna, a myna," said Kado to himself. "Perhaps if I am careful I can catch that myna bird. I will make a cage for it and teach it to talk to me. I will teach it the chant of the charm doctor, and it can drive the evil spirits and the snakes away from our house."

Kado arose cautiously to his feet and saw the myna perched on a low branch. Kado could almost touch it with his hand. Then he thought of his gourd of rice. Perhaps he could coax the bird to come closer so he could catch it by the legs. Placing a bit of rice on a lower branch, Kado waited. The myna continued to make queer sounds, but did not venture near. Kado was very patient. How much he wanted that myna! Other boys of the village had mynas and parrots. They taught them to talk. What fun he and his brothers would have if only—

The myna came closer and began to peck at the rice. Kado reached up, but the bird spread its wings and flew to a nearby tree. Kado was not discouraged. He determined to catch that bird if it took all morning. Following slowly and carefully, Kado placed more rice where the bird could see it. Again the myna slipped out of Kado's reach, flew out over the valley, and perched on a rock. Keeping his eyes on the myna, yet watching always for signs of danger, Kado followed the bird across the valley. He placed a bit of rice on the rock and waited. The myna came closer, pecked at the rice, then suddenly flew away. Kado watched it circling overhead. Then he heard a sound that made him lose all interest in the myna. From over the hill he heard a call that sent chills of fear into his heart. It was the shout of "TIGER, TIGER!"

At that call, the natives gather in groups, or run home as fast as they can, shouting the warning to others. Kado did not care for the myna now. In his mind he did not see a dark bird with yellow bill, and wings with white tips. No, he saw a huge tiger, with black and orange stripes, and powerful, sharp claws! His one thought was to get back safely to mother and his brothers, and the group of wood gatherers. So he hurried across the valley, away from the direction from which the call came.

When he came to the clearing where he thought they would be, they were not there! "Mother, mother!" he called, running frantically down one path and back on another. "Mother, Tari! Where are you?"

There was no answer. Again he called; but only the ominous call of "Tiger, tiger!" echoed through the forest. Kado tried to think of the chant of the charm doctor, but there was no time now for that. He must rejoin the wood gatherers, for there was a hungry tiger somewhere near in the jungle. Someone had seen it, someone had called to give warning.

Kado was sure that each new path he chose would lead him to mother. But after running until he was quite out of breath he realized that he was lost. The myna circled over his head, making a queer noise. Kado thought that it also was calling "Tiger, tiger!" Then everything became quiet. Kado paused a moment to catch his breath. He was trembling with fear. It seemed as if the jungle were closing in around him. He thought he could see tiger eyes peering at him in every direction. Then he heard voices. They seemed to be from a wooded knoll ahead of him.

"Mother, mother," called Kado, as he ran from the ferocious tiger. The boy thought he could see the orange-and-black animal peering at him.

"Mother, mother!" he called, running in the direction of the welcome sounds. Soon he would be safe from the tiger, safe with mother and his three brothers. He ran up the hill. How good it was to see people among the trees. Then Kado stopped suddenly in the path. Mother and his three brothers were not there. This was not his group of wood gatherers; these people were different. They were not from his village, for they dressed differently. The leader did not have brown skin. Kado opened his eyes wide in wonder. Could it be that he was the missionary?

Kado wanted to turn and run, but the shouts of "Tiger, tiger!" continued to echo through the trees. He dared not leave the shelter of a group of people to face a tiger. Or was a tiger more to be feared than a missionary? It was difficult to decide, but the boy finally chose to stay with the people. He followed close behind them as they went deeper into the forest. Coming out into a clearing on the other side of a hill, Kado followed them out across the valley, over a little bridge, and up a long trail over a wooded hill, and into another valley.

Kado became tired and hot. His bare feet seemed to burn on the hot stones along the way. He felt lonely and lost as he followed the men and boys until they came into a clearing. What he saw there made him blink, rub his eyes, and blink again. Nestled among the trees and bushes were large buildings with red-tiled roofs and many windows. He had never seen anything like this before.

"Dreamland," said Kado to himself, yet he knew it was not a dream. He was very much awake. He felt of his hatchet within the folds of his garment. His gourd of rice and curry was still hanging from the fiber cord around his neck. His feet were sore and tired, and his heart was pounding inside his chest with a strange mixture of fear and loneliness.

For a moment he stood looking at the scene before him and at the strange people he had followed. He suddenly realized that this was the mission where people became Christians, where boys went to school to learn a trade. Here they learned to care for their bodies and be clean. They learned to read and write, and they helped the missionary doctor care for sick people. One of those long buildings must be the hospital where sick people were taken to be treated for snake bites, fevers, cuts, and burns. Kado had never been taken to the mission hospital, for his parents were not Christians. They worshiped monkeys, spirits, and devil gods.

Kado looked with wonder at the buildings before him and said to himself, "I am afraid to be here. I am afraid of the missionary and the Christians. They will cast a spell on me and make me a Christian, too. I cannot stay here. But how will I ever find my way home? I am so far away from home and mother."

Big tears welled up in Kado's eyes. He brushed them away with the back of his little brown hand. He found a place of shelter between some bushes. He was far enough away from the Christians, yet near enough in case the tiger came. Surely they would protect him from the tiger, even though they were Christians.

KADO SEES STRANGE SIGHTS

THE sun was high in the sky when Kado heard a drum not far away. It startled Kado, but he remained motionless behind the bushes. From all around, it seemed, boys came running. They gathered in front of one of the long buildings. Then as the missionary beckoned to them, they all disappeared inside the big door.

Although he had been taught to fear the mission as much as he feared the snakes and wild beasts of the jungle, Kado was curious to know what was going on behind that big door. Creeping cautiously from bush to bush, he crouched down beneath an open window. He heard strange noises, he smelled food. Of course, it was dinnertime! Kado peered over the window sill and saw the boys seated on benches beside long tables, conveying strange food from round plates to their mouths by means of sharp pointed metal instruments. The missionary was at the end of the table doing the same thing. He was speaking to the boys, giving instructions, and telling of plans for the afternoon's work, which would follow the noon rest period.

The smell of food reminded Kado that he, too, was hungry. He felt of his little gourd. Yes, it was still there. He had not given all the rice to the myna. Slipping back to the shelter of the bushes, Kado sat down and ate his rice and curry, using only his brown hand to take it from the gourd up to his mouth. After he had eaten his dinner, he felt drowsy. It was a hot day, but how could he go to sleep when there was so much to see?

Soon the boys came out of the building, and each one found a place to relax and rest in the shade. Habit and nature have a strange way with people's lives. The day was very warm. Soon, in spite of his efforts to stay awake, Kado found himself drifting off to sleep under the big bush near the mission.

When he awoke he thought he still must be in dreamland, but then he remembered how he had followed the missionary and a group of Christian boys. During the afternoon, Kado watched the various activities around the mission school. He saw some of the boys cutting the grass on the lawn. Others were trimming trees and hedges. Older boys were making things with boards, hammers, and saws. Some were weaving reed mats and baskets.

In one of the buildings Kado heard sounds of reading. He heard students reciting lessons and singing. That must be the school, he thought. Kado wondered what was in the other long building to the left. Once he saw the missionary, dressed all in white, go in there. He saw people going in and coming out. Then Kado saw two native boys carrying a man on a stretcher between them. A crowd had gathered and was following behind the stretcher. Kado heard the words "snake bite," "swelling," "will die in a few minutes."

Kado became more curious. Finally, he took courage and stood with the crowd near the door while the missionary came out to examine the poor man on the stretcher. Kado had seen it happen before. When a man had been bitten on the ankle by a poisonous snake, his leg would swell up, and in a short time the man would die. It was a common occurrence in the jungle.

Kado used his eyes and his ears. He did not miss anything. The missionary was speaking to the two boys who carried the stretcher.

"Good boys, Tim and Orlo. You have made good time. Bring the man right in, and we'll do what we can."

The patient was laid on a clean white bed. The people stood outside the door watching to see what the missionary would do. Kado stood near enough to see, too. The missionary quickly prepared some magic water in a little bottle. Then, before he did anything more, he said, "We will pray to the God in heaven."

Kado listened. The people standing near the door listened. Tim and Orlo stood with hands folded, and eyes closed, listening to the missionary doctor as he prayed to the God in heaven. There were no weird chants, no charms, no rattling of shells and bones. It was a simple prayer, asking that the man who had received the snake bite might now receive the blessing of healing from the God in heaven.

Then the missionary doctor went to work. With his magic needle and the magic water, he soothed the patient to a quiet rest. Then with his little knife, he skillfully cut into the snake bite and drew the poison out with medicine on bits of cotton. The patient did not stir. Kado thought he was dead. But the people who stood watching had confidence in the missionary doctor, and they said, "He will not die; he will get well. The God in heaven will make him well."

This was a new experience for Kado. He did not know about the God in heaven. Kado stood by the door, gazing in awe at the bottles and instruments in the glass case on the wall. He watched the missionary moving about. He saw the smiles of confidence and assurance that he gave Tim and Orlo and the people standing near the door. Finally, the people went away, and Kado went back to his hiding place in the bushes. He was afraid the missionary might speak to him. That would surely mean that he, too, would become a Christian, and that would only bring disaster to his family back home. The spirits would be angry and bring a curse on his father and mother and his three brothers.

KADO HEARS A NEW SONG

SOON the evening shadows began to grow long in the valley. People from the village gathered in the mission yard and sat in rows around the missionary. Kado was curious to know what it was all about. He wanted to see the pictures and hear the stories the missionary was telling. Kado listened wide-eyed as the missionary told of the God in heaven and of Jesus, God's gift to man, who came to do good to all men and to heal those who would come to Him. Then Kado opened his eyes even wider. The people sat quietly as the mission lady began to sing. She had a sweet voice and a kind face. Surely one would not need to fear a lady as sweet and kind as she. Kado thought of his own mother who was sweet and kind, too.

Kado listened to the words of the song that the mission lady was singing. It was about Jesus and His love.

> *I will tell you why I love the Saviour,*
> *Why my love for Him is full and free:*
> *He came down to earth to save the sinner,*
> *Now I love, because He first loved me.*

CHORUS:

> *Oh, yes, I love Jesus, for He first loved me,*
> *Yes, I love Jesus, for He died for me,*
> *For it was on Calvary, Jesus died to save me,*
> *Oh, yes, I love Jesus, for He first loved me.*

Kado was interested in seeing the pictures of Jesus and in singing about His love. When the song was ended the boy had a very strange feeling.

I will tell how on the cross they nailed Him,
Yet He rose triumphant from the grave;
Now He is in heaven, interceding,
Pleading for the ones He died to save.

Soon He's coming back in all His glory,
Coming in the glory of a King,
Coming to redeem the ones who love Him;
That is why I love His praise to sing.

When the song was ended, Kado had a strange feeling inside his breast. He was no longer afraid of the missionary or the mission lady. He was not afraid of the Christian boys he had followed to the valley. That song had done something to Kado. Now he wanted to know more about Jesus.

The people begged for more stories and more songs. They listened attentively to every word, and Kado listened, too. It was all so new and strange. Then the missionary asked everyone to stand, and he prayed that the God in heaven would protect them and keep them all safe during the dark night. Kado somehow felt that he was included in that prayer.

As Kado stood watching the people leave for their homes in the village, he felt a gentle hand on his shoulder. He turned and looked up into the kind eyes and sweet face of the mission lady. She had a roll of bandages in one hand. She paused to say, "Good night, boy. I hope you sleep well, and may the God in heaven protect you during the night." With a tender, motherly smile, and a friendly pat, she was gone.

As Kado watched her disappear within the door of the hospital, a sudden fear came over him. The mission lady had spoken to him; she had touched him. Then the feeling was changed to homesickness. He was lost; he was far, far away from home and loved ones. How he wanted his own mother! With a sob he burst into tears and ran to the shelter of the big bush. But he did not stay long beside the big bush. It had sheltered and hidden him from sight during the day, but it would not be safe to remain there during the night. Suddenly Kado spied a tree near the hospital. It had large spreading branches and there were friendly lights nearby. The missionary was there. The mission lady, who had sung that song about Jesus, was near.

Kado climbed up into the tree by holding firmly to the branches above him. He sat on a low branch, where he could see into one of the hospital windows. He saw the missionary moving about, putting bottles upon a shelf on the wall. He saw the mission lady putting a clean bandage on the ankle of the man who had been treated for snake bite. The man was still alive. The God in heaven did not let him die. All during the night Kado sat up in the tree. The boy heard strange night sounds all around him; but he felt safe in the tree. He thought of the mission lady and of the song she sang. He called it the "Jesus Song."

"Someday I hope to learn to sing that song, too," said Kado to himself. "I want to know more about Jesus. I want to learn to trust in the God in heaven."

KADO AND THE MAGIC NEEDLE

FOR a long time Kado sat in the tree, watching the activities in the mission hospital. The missionary doctor faithfully watched the patient who lay so still on the clean white bed. All was quiet except for the strange night sounds of the jungle. Kado became drowsy, for it was long past his bedtime. He was hungry, too, for his little rice gourd hung empty from its cord around his neck. Now and then he nodded, but then quickly aroused himself and clung more firmly to the branches above him. He tried hard to keep awake, but all in vain. He fell asleep, and then quite suddenly he awoke as he felt himself falling to the ground. His scream of fright was lost in a period of unconsciousness.

When Kado awoke it was daylight, and he looked around him. He was lying on one of the white cots in the hospital. The missionary doctor was standing near, taking medicine from a bottle. The magic needle was on a tray beside him. The kind mission lady was bending over him. She smiled as Kado opened his eyes.

"Everything will soon be all right, boy," she said, patting his brown arm.

"Where? How?" began Kado, trying to rise. A sharp pain in his shoulder caused him to wince and lie back.

"Now lie still," said the mission lady gently. "You must have been sleeping in the tree outside the window, and you fell. The doctor heard you scream, and he carried you in here to see how badly you were hurt. Your shoulder is severely bruised, but there are no bones broken.

He will give you some medicine with his magic needle that will make you feel better."

Somehow Kado did not feel afraid when the missionary doctor injected the magic needle containing the magic water into his arm. The mission lady gently swabbed the place with a bit of cotton, then asked, "Tell me, boy, how did it happen that you slept in that tree? Why did you not go home after the meeting was over?"

Kado then told his story: how he had become lost from the wood gatherers while chasing a myna.

"And you stayed here at the mission all day?" asked the mission lady. "Then you did not have any supper. You must be very hungry."

Kado nodded and pointed to his empty rice gourd. The mission lady left the room.

The doctor went about his work, taking care of the other patients. The man with the snake bite was much better. He was talking to the missionary, telling how grateful he was for the magic needle.

"It was more than the magic needle that saved your life," said the missionary doctor. "Without the help of the God in heaven, the things we did would have been useless."

Kado listened. It was all so new and strange.

Soon the mission lady returned with a tempting bowl of rice and some fruit. Kado thanked her graciously, and proceeded to eat. He was hungry, and it tasted good.

KADO RETURNS HOME

THE missionary doctor kept Kado at the hospital to rest for a few hours. Later in the morning the doctor said, "In a little while I am going in the oxcart to your village. If you wish, I will take you with me. I am sure your parents must be worried about you. I think you have rested enough to be able to travel."

Kado thanked the mission lady for her kindness to him. Then he added, "Thank you for singing the Jesus song last night. Someday I want to learn to sing it, too."

The oxcart slowly bumped along the dusty trail. The missionary told Kado many things as they rode along. He told him about the mission and the school, and how the boys learned to become strong, clean, and useful citizens to serve their fellow men. Kado was quietly thinking. So many things had happened to him in a few short hours. The pain in his shoulder was still there, though it was not so severe as it had been. The magic water was doing its work. Now he was on his way back to his own village, riding with the missionary doctor in the oxcart.

As they neared the village, Kado recognized many familiar sights. How good it seemed to be coming home. Yet he felt he had been among friends at the mission. They had been very kind to him, and he no longer feared them.

As they came to a fork in the road, Kado said, "I can go across the field here. My home is just beyond that little

As they came to the fork in the road, Kado got out and said good-by to the missionary doctor. The boy remembered the days at the mission.

hill. Thank you for the ride and for everything—even the magic needle."

The boy got down from the oxcart and started across the field. The missionary was soon out of sight behind a clump of trees. Kado followed a familiar trail. How good it seemed to be home.

The sun was setting like a great round red ball over the lotus pool as Kado came up the little path to his home. He could smell the smoke of the fire between the stones in the corner where the kettle of rice was cooking. The family was ready to eat their evening meal as Kado entered the door.

"Kado!" they cried in chorus. "We thought you had been taken by the tiger! Where have you been? We have been searching all day for you."

Then Kado told about all his adventures. Tari, Lesso, and Con gazed at him in wide-eyed amazement as he told of his fall from the tree and of how the missionary doctor used the magic needle on his arm. They all looked at the tiny hole where the magic water went in. Father and mother listened carefully. They looked at each other, then back at Kado.

"Don't ever let the charm doctor know about this," said father. "If he ever found out that the missionary and his wife even spoke to you, he would be very angry. He might put a dreadful curse upon us. What would he do if he knew they had fed you and had given you magic water through a magic needle? Oh, Kado, my son! How could you do this to us!"

Father was angry, and mother was displeased because Kado had wandered away from the wood gatherers.

"I know it was my fault," said Kado. "I should not have followed the myna, but I tried to find the way back.

When I heard the call 'Tiger, tiger!' I got lost. I did not want to be lost."

"We are glad you found your way back to us, Kado," said mother tenderly. "Now let us all go to sleep. It will soon be morning again, and there is much to do."

Mother put away the remnants of supper while the boys spread their garments upon the floor. Soon father and mother and Kado's three brothers were fast asleep, but Kado could not sleep. For a long time he lay on his little pallet on the floor. It was good to be home, but he did not like to have his father angry with him.

Kado buried his face in his garment and cried. He must not waken father and mother. They were tired from working and searching for him. They needed rest.

There was still pain in his shoulder, but there was a greater pain in his heart. He would be the one to blame if trouble came to his family because of this experience. Surely if father and mother could have seen the mission, and heard the missionary speak, they would have a different opinion of Christians. If they could only hear the mission lady sing that song!

Kado looked out of the little door. He saw the moon sailing through the fleecy clouds, high over the jungle trees. Somewhere up there in the sky was the God in heaven that the missionary told about. Somewhere beyond the twinkling stars was the Jesus the mission lady sang about. Kado tried to recall the words of the song.

If he only knew more about the things he had learned that day at the mission. If he could only sing the Jesus song!

The moon seemed to smile as the tired eyes of the brown boy closed. Kado was fast asleep.

KADO AND THE SPOTTED LEOPARD

HOW long Kado had been asleep, he did not know. When he awoke, the moon was still smiling in the sky, hiding now and then behind a fleecy cloud. The friendly stars still twinkled. Kado sat up on his pallet. He thought he heard a noise out in the enclosure behind the house.There was a strange commotion among the cattle. Kado awakened father, and he in turn awakened the other boys. They armed themselves with sticks and clubs that were always kept beside the door in case of intruders. They ran quickly to see what was happening to disturb the cows. As they approached they saw a huge spotted leopard leap over the wall of the enclosure, taking one of the calves with it. There was no sound. Leopards move swiftly and silently. Father and the boys let out a loud yell to frighten the leopard. They scrambled over the wall, thinking to rescue the calf, but they could find neither the calf nor the leopard. Both had disappeared in the tangled brush beyond.

"The spirits are angry," said father, as he turned to go back to the house. "They have sent a curse upon us. I knew it would come! The spirits are angry."

Silently they went back into the house, placed their sticks and clubs in the corner by the door, and lay down again. Kado wished that he could do something to break the spell so father would not be angry with him. He was sorry to lose the calf. Why should the spotted leopards eat little calves? Why did the God in heaven let some animals hurt others, if He made all the animals?

Could it be true what the missionary said that the God in heaven was stronger and more powerful than any spirits, gods, or devils? The misionary had said that it was the evil powers that caused snakes to bite people. The missionary was kind. He used the magic needle and medicines out of bottles to help make people well. Why, then, should one fear the missionaries and Christians? It was all confusing to Kado. It was hard for him to think that kind people like the missionary doctor and the mission lady were to be feared as enemies. They were kind; they prayed to the God in heaven. They sang the Jesus song.

As Kado watched the stars and the moon, he had a longing to go back to the mission in the valley. "I want to go to school to learn to help people. I want to learn to read and work as do Tim and Orlo. I, too, want to be a Christian. I want to worship the God in heaven and sing the Jesus song."

Morning came. It was time to get up, eat breakfast, and go to work. Father was cross, and he seemed to blame Kado for the loss of the calf.

"We must work all the harder now, son," he said as he took up his gourd of rice and started across the field with his sons following close behind him. It was another hot day. Kado worked faithfully, digging out roots and hoeing in the fields. He tried to be cheerful as he worked with Tari, Lesso, and Con; but his heart was heavy and his shoulder ached. He was glad when father looked up toward the sun and said, "Dinnertime, boys."

They followed father, and all sat under a big shade tree. They enjoyed their curry and rice from the gourds. Father did not say much during the few moments while they ate their dinner. Kado thought that he must still be angry. The sun seemed hotter than ever as they went back to work in the fields. Many times during the long afternoon Kado wanted to rest. He was weary, but he kept on because of the experience of the calf and the spotted leopard.

"Tell us more, Kado," said Tari, when the boys were at the opposite side of the field from their father. "Tell us more about the mission. We will not tell father that you told us. Tell us more about the God in heaven."

In low tones Kado told his three brothers many things that he had not mentioned the night before. It was all so new to Kado that he felt he could not do justice to what he had seen and heard.

"If I only knew more, so I could tell you," said Kado. "If I could only go to the mission school to learn!'

"Father would never let you go," said Lesso. "He needs you to help in the fields."

"But after the rice harvest is over, there is not so much to do."

"Would you have to be a Christian if you went to the mission?" asked Con.

"I do not know," answered Kado. "But I do know that the Christians are not what the charm doctor says. We must not talk now; father is coming toward us across the field."

That night, while the family gathered around the bowl of rice and beans, Kado dared to ask, "Father, after the rice harvest is over, will you need me here to help? The boys are getting to be good workers now. Even little Con kept up with me today, and Tari and Lesso are big and strong."

"What do you plan to do, son, when the rice harvest is over?"

"I want to go to school down at the mission."

35

Father said, "No!" Then after a moment of painful silence he said, "It would cost many rupees."

"I know," said Kado, "but many of the boys who go there are also poor. They may work at the mission to pay their way. Some cut grass, trim trees, saw boards to to make things, or weave mats and baskets to sell. I would work hard if I could go and learn, father."

Mother seemed quite interested. She, too, had been thinking all day. She thought of the experience in the forest, and how her grief at losing her Kado had turned to joy at his return. Did not the missionary bring him back to her? In the forest she had prayed to all the gods she had been taught to worship, but they had not brought him back to her. Surely the hungry tiger had taken her son, she thought, for he could not be found. Then, in her secret heart she had prayed to the God in heaven. She did not dare let the spirits know she had even thought that prayer. She had asked the God in heaven to find Kado. Then the missionary had brought him back to the village. Perhaps the God in heaven did answer her prayer.

"I think it would be good for Kado to go," said mother. "He will learn many things at the mission that we cannot teach him here. He will learn to make things and to be of more help to his father. Yes, I think Kado should go to the mission when the rice harvest is over." And strange to say, father agreed.

That night Kado curled up on his mat and quickly went to sleep, for his body was tired and his shoulder ached. He had worked hard all day. Even though his body was tired, his heart was happy. He could now make plans to go to the mission school if they would take him in. He would learn to read and write, and work with his hands. He would learn about the God in heaven and sing the Jesus song.

KADO AND THE COOKY JAR

KADO stood in the kitchen doorway of the mission house, tired and hungry. He had walked for miles through a dangerous part of the country from his home village. He was clothed in the simple dress of the natives of India, a wrap-around garment with a red fringe in front. His brown body was dusty and scratched.

He greeted the missionary's wife politely and asked in his native tongue, "Please, may I come to your school? I know I am poor, and my parents have no money to pay you; but I will work hard. I will scrub for you. I will do anything, only let me go to school so I can learn about Jesus. I want to learn the Jesus song."

The yearning in his voice and the earnest look in his deep brown eyes won the heart of the mission lady. How could she refuse him a place in a Christian school when he was so sincere to know more about the better things of life? She looked down into the eyes of the boy. He was hungry for food as well as knowledge. She must not turn him away; she must give him food for all his needs.

"Sit down, boy," she said, and her voice betrayed the love and sympathy she felt in her heart. She set a bowl of rice and curry before him, and he ate hungrily. Then she took some cookies from the cooky jar on the kitchen shelf, and while he ate them she told him the story of Jesus. It was the sweet story told in a simple way he could understand. Kado learned of the Babe in the manger, of the Man who went about doing good, of the

The boy stood at the door of the mission house, dressed in simple native clothes. He looked tired as he said, "Please, may I come to your school?"

Saviour on the cross, and of the Redeemer who is coming soon.

The boy listened, eagerly drinking in every word. His heart was touched. Here, indeed, was good ground for the precious seeds of truth. There were tears in Kado's eyes as the woman finished the story.

"Now will you sing me the Jesus song?" he asked.

The little kitchen seemed filled with sunlight as she sang softly and sweetly the song she loved, the song Kado had been longing to hear—the Jesus song. His heart echoed the words. He hummed the simple melody with her, trying to learn it.

Kado proved to be a diligent and willing worker. He was faithful to the tasks assigned him. His brown face shone with a new light as the Jesus story was unfolded to him day by day in the classroom. He learned to sing the Jesus song, and he sang it every day as he worked.

One morning Kado was down on his knees scrubbing the kitchen floor of the mission house. The mission lady was working in the adjoining room, which was separated from the kitchen by heavy drapes. Kado was singing the Jesus song as usual as he worked.

Suddenly all was still in the kitchen, the singing stopped. The mission lady thought she heard the lid of the cooky jar rattle. Perhaps Kado was hungry, and seeing the cooky jar so near him on the shelf, had decided to help himself to one of her cookies. Well, he was welcome to it. She had planned to give him some when he finished scrubbing, but she would rather have him ask for things he wanted than to take them without asking.

The song began again. Kado continued scrubbing. The mission lady dismissed the incident from her mind, thinking only of the marked change that had taken place in the life of the brown boy since she had taken him into the school.

Then the singing stopped again, and once more the lid of the cooky jar was lifted. Then the Jesus song was sung as Kado continued his task. The mission lady drew the drapes aside a tiny crack so she could watch Kado. She would have to speak to him about it if he did it again, for she wanted him to learn the lesson of respect for other people's things.

Kado was on his knees, scrubbing vigorously. The muscles in his brown body were strong and active. His voice was clear and vibrant as he sang his favorite song.

Suddenly he stopped singing. He laid aside the cleaning cloth. The mission lady silently watched him through the parted drapes. The moment she had anticipated had come.

Kado folded his hands and closed his eyes. For a brief moment he was in an attitude of prayer. Then he arose from his knees, went to the shelf, took a cooky from the jar, and replaced the lid. Then, to the mission lady's surprise, instead of eating it, he tucked the cooky in the folds of his wrap-around garment and went back to his scrubbing, singing the Jesus song.

She was puzzled. What did it mean? How could he steal cookies, yet pray and sing the Jesus song? Had not her teaching found its rightful place in his heart? She continued watching him. Twice more the incident was repeated, while the mission lady watched. When the kitchen floor was finished, Kado arose from his knees to put the scrub pail and cleaning things away. The mission lady came out into the kitchen. She must speak to him about the cookies. She would be tactful, yet firm. Before she could say anything to him, however, Kado announced, "I am going back to my village."

That meant he had not completely won the victory after all. He was going back, to the worship of monkeys and devil gods with his family. Had the teaching and the influence of the mission school been only in vain?

Her voice trembled as she asked, "Are you sure, Kado, that you really want to return to the village?"

"Oh, I must go back," he said decidedly. "I just can't stay here another day. The scrubbing is all done. I will go right now. It is a long way back to my village; if I hurry I will be there before dark."

"I am sorry you feel you must leave us, Kado. If I had known you were leaving so soon, I would have given you a lunch to take along. You did not need to steal the cookies. I would gladly have given them to you if you had asked me."

"Oh, I will put them all back in the cooky jar," said Kado, starting to remove them from the folds of his garment. "I didn't know I was stealing them."

The mission lady could see the shapes of the round disks under the cloth—two on one side, and three on the other. But he must not put them back into the cooky jar after they had been between the folds of his garment.

"Oh, no, Kado," she said quickly, "do not put them back into the jar. You may keep them to eat as you take your long journey back to your village."

Kado looked up into her eyes. Evidently she had misunderstood his motive in taking the five cookies. She had always been so kind to him. Couldn't she know what was in his heart that prompted him to take them? Didn't she read it in his eyes that his love for Jesus would not let him steal?

"Oh, they are not for me to eat," said Kado, holding out his hands for mercy. "I did not take them for myself. These two," he said, as he patted the two round disks on his left side, "are for my father and mother. And the three on this side are for my three brothers. I prayed that my people will no longer worship monkeys and the devil gods, and that they, too, will learn to sing the Jesus song. But there is no mission in my village, and they will never know the story of Jesus unless I tell them. I am taking these cookies, one to each, so that I may tell them about Jesus as you told me while I ate cookies. I must hurry back to my village. I will sing the Jesus song to my people. I know it is a long way and full of danger; but I am not afraid. I will come back in time for class on Monday."

There were tears, in the eyes of the mission lady. Her heart was too happy for words. She took Kado's outstretched hand in hers and patted it gently as she whispered a prayer, "Forgive me, dear Father, for my lack of faith."

Then aloud she said, "Go, Kado, and may God keep you safe and bless you as you sing the Jesus song to your people."

She gave the boy a packet of lunch to eat along the way, including several cookies. As she watched him disappear into the bushes, she said softly, "A light to those who sit in darkness. How brightly that light will shine as he sings the Jesus song to his people!"

KADO AND THE TIGER

KADO hurried along the dusty trail toward home. In his hand he carried the precious bag of cookies that the mission lady had given him. He would take them to his father and mother and three brothers. Kado had been to the mission school only a few weeks; but already he knew the story of Jesus, and he could sing the Jesus song. Now he wanted his parents to love Jesus, too.

It was late in the afternoon when Kado reached the wooded section which bordered his village. His feet were tired, and he was hot and dusty; but he hurried on, for he wanted to reach home before dark. As he came to a bend in the road, he heard a familiar sound—the squeaking wheels of his father's oxcart. He hurried even faster in order to overtake it, and he eagerly scrambled up beside father on the load of supplies.

Kado beamed with delight to see his father again, and his father seemed equally glad to see him. Kado's face shone with a new light as he told him all about the mission school. Father could see how clean and happy he looked. Maybe the Christian school was not so bad after all, even if they did worship a different God.

"What do you have in the bag, Kado?" he asked, looking curiously at the bag that Kado held in his hand.

"Something for you and mother and the boys," he said proudly.

"What is it?" asked father.

After Kado had scrambled onto the cart with his father he opened a sack. "I have something for you and Mother and the boys," he said.

Kado hesitated a moment. He remembered something that the mission lady had read to the class from the Bible: "Behold, now is the accepted time." He would tell him now, while they were plodding along home. He would tell him about God and Jesus, and sing the Jesus song. So he opened the brown bag and took out one of the cookies for father.

Kado's father had never before tasted cookies such as the mission lady baked. He licked his lips after eating the cooky and looked wistfully at the brown bag in Kado's hand; but Kado said, "These are for mother and the boys. But I will give you one of mine." The boy pulled a rather crumpled cooky from the folds of his wrap-around garment and gave it to his father. Then he told him the story of Jesus and sang the Jesus song.

Father listened carefully to every word. As he looked at the golden sky where the sun was setting he almost believed in the God who created the heavens and the earth. Could it be that God loved him, too? Did God send His only Son to die for him?

It was dark by the time they came out into the clearing. They could barely see the dim trail, but the oxen knew the way and were anxious to get home. Kado's father was thoughtful. If the mission school had done this much for Kado, perhaps he should send the other boys. If only he could have faith in the God of heaven.

Suddenly the oxen stopped! No matter how much they were coaxed and prodded, they would not go on. They nervously twisted and tried to back up. They made a queer sound in their throats, and stared straight ahead at some dark object in the road.

Kado and his father peered into the shadows. Fear clutched their hearts when they realized it was a huge tiger crouching in the darkness, his tall lashing from side to side.

"If we turn back, it will spring at us," whispered father hoarsely. "We certainly cannot go on. What shall we do?"

"We can pray," whispered Kado, gently pressing his father's arm. "Pray, father, pray to the God in heaven, while I sing the Jesus song."

With hands reverently folded over the cooky bag, and his eyes tightly closed, Kado prayed for help. Then he started singing the Jesus song. Father kept his eyes on the shadowy figure in the road. His heart was stirred as the sweet, boyish voice told of the love of Jesus. Kado was singing the song he loved. Kado believed that the God in heaven was "a very present help in trouble."

Suddenly the oxen started, jerking the cart into motion. The wheels of the oxcart squeaked. Straight ahead the oxen went again, toward home. Kado's father peered into the shadows. The tiger was gone!

"I knew God would help us," said Kado. "The tiger went away while we were praying. The mission lady told us always to pray when we are in trouble, and God will send His angels as He did for Daniel when he was in a den of lions! This was just one tiger."

When Kado and his father arrived home, supper was ready. Mother and the three brothers greeted the returning boy warmly. He was glad to be home again. Father was thoughtful as he gathered with his family around the bowl of rice. He listened as Kado gave thanks to God for the humble food and for their miraculous deliverance from the tiger.

After supper, Kado gave out the remaining cookies. Then he told the the story of Jesus as the mission lady had told it to him. When he taught his mother and brothers to sing the Jesus song, father sang it with him.

Then father announced, "From now on we, too, will worship and pray to the God of heaven. We will always sing the Jesus song. If there is room at the mission school, I will send my three younger sons that they, too, may have the faith that Kado has."

KADO'S BROTHERS

THE SQUEAKING oxcart rolled slowly toward the mission station. In the cart were Kado's father and mother, his three brothers, Tari, Lesso, and Con, and the few family possessions, including cooking utensils and bedding. They had sold their home in the village and were moving nearer to the mission school, where the boys could learn more about Jesus. Father would work harder than ever now that he had the purpose in life of giving his boys a Christian education.

Kado had already gone back to the mission school. He had waited many days for his family to come. His father had made arrangements for the three brothers to become students at the school.

The day came when the brothers started attending classes with Kado. They were eager to learn and were willing pupils. Day by day the influence of the school made impressions on their young lives. They, too, learned to sing the Jesus song.

Then one day Kado overheard a conversation that made his heart sad. Little things had been disappearing from the school from time to time; sometimes they were returned, sometimes they were not. Suspicion pointed to the three brothers, who had been seen sneaking through the brush late in the evening.

"I can't believe they would do it," Kado confided to the mission lady. "I am sure that they love Jesus. I have prayed for them. Will you speak to them? You know what to say in the nice way, and they will listen to you."

"Of course it is just a suspicion, Kado. We will wait until we know it is your brothers who have been taking things before we talk to them. Meanwhile, we will continue to pray that they will do right."

With a heavy heart, Kado went about his tasks, trying to hide the tears that welled up into his eyes. His brothers seemed to adjust themselves to the school in every way, and they loved to sing the Jesus song.

Kado wondered what had been taken. Someone must have been mistaken. Surely his brothers would not steal. Tari was a good boy. Lesso and Con were sometimes full of mischief, but they would not take things that did not belong to them.

Kado was silent during the evening meal. The food seemed to choke him when he tried to swallow. He looked across the rice bowl at Lesso and Con. They were evidently enjoying their food, for they were smiling and exchanging pleasant conversation. Tari was quite thoughtful as he ate; he seemed to be a bit uneasy.

When it was quite dark, Kado made preparations for bed. But the three brothers were nowhere to be seen. Kado called to them in the darkness, but there was no reply. Neither father nor mother knew where they had gone. Kado lay awake a long time on his pallet, thinking and praying. He prayed that God would guide his brothers safely home. There were many dangers in the night, but one of the greatest dangers is sin. To steal is a sin.

Kado listened. He thought he heard singing. Yes, it was the Jesus song. Since Tari's voice was deeper than the others, he added the bass quality to the trio. The three brothers were returning from their nightly adventure.

Kado decided he would say nothing. While they made preparations for the night, he pretended to be sound asleep. But tomorrow night he would solve the mystery by following them.

The next night, immediately after supper, Kado kept his eyes on Tari. For several minutes he busied himself with his personal appearance. This was a new trait that had developed since the boys had entered school.

At a signal from Tari, Lesso and Con went outside and disappeared in the darkness. Tari spoke a few words to his father, and then the third brother went out. Kado followed close behind him, slipping between bushes and vines until he came to the open road. Kado's heart beat rapidly as he realized that Tari was going toward the mission school. Were his brothers guilty after all?

Silently Kado followed, keeping well back in the shadows. He must not be seen. Tari paused but a moment near the mission house. There was no sound but the night insects, yet Kado's heart was filled with fear. Across the yard Tari went, disappearing in the bushes beyond. Kado followed, forgetting the dangers of the night if he could only help his brothers.

Suddenly Kado stopped. Before him was a little clearing, a sheltered spot where a campfire blazed. The moon shone down on a scene which made Kado's heart almost miss a beat. There in a circle around the campfire sat nearly twenty native boys, dirty and scantily dressed. As Tari approached, the boys looked up. Kado recognized Lesso and Con in the group. What was this, a band of robbers waiting only for a signal from their leader to begin a raid?

Kado crouched behind a tree, listening and watching. All eyes were on Tari as he talked in subdued tones. Kado was too far away to hear what he was saying. He dared not come nearer for fear of being seen.

Then, to Kado's surprise, they began to sing the Jesus song. Kado listened. How he loved that song! It had become a part of his life. But this was not the time or place to sing *that* song. Didn't they know, couldn't they realize, that Jesus did not want them to steal? Kado closed his eyes and breathed a prayer. When he opened them again, he could scarcely believe what he saw. Around the campfire were twenty brown boys, kneeling in prayer. Tari, Lesso, and Con each said a few words; then they all repeated the Lord's Prayer in their native language.

This was almost too much for Kado. He watched as Lesso and Con brought out a worn picture roll that had been discarded long ago as worthless. They unrolled it and held it between them so that the firelight could shine upon its fragments. Tari began telling stories while the boys gathered closer, eagerly drinking in every word. Tari's face shone with enthusiasm as he told the stories as he had heard the mission lady tell them to the class. Kado longed to join them; but, no, he would wait. It might spoil it all if he made his appearance. Kado was proud of his brothers. They were letting their light shine.

When all the pictures had been explained, and many questions had been answered, the boys were still eager for more.

"Tomorrow night," promised Tari, "we'll have more." The boys sang another song, and then stood in a circle with bowed heads. Afterward they smothered the campfire and slipped away into the night, leaving the three brothers to put the precious fragments of the picture roll in a safe place.

Kado lingered a moment after the brothers had gone. He went over to the spot where the campfire had burned. He felt as Moses must have felt when he stood before the burning bush—he was on holy ground. In a

In the flickering light of the jungle fire sat a group of
eager-faced boys listening to Tari as he told the stories he had
heard at the mission.

few moments he started for home. He knew he could find his way, even though the path wound in and out among the bushes. When he came to the mission house he saw a light burning in the study room. Timidly knocking on the outer door, Kado waited.

"Is anything wrong, Kado?" asked the mission lady anxiously. "You should have been asleep long ago."

"I had to tell you tonight. It is not my brothers who are taking things," said Kado. Then he told what he had seen and heard around the campfire. He told the lady about the worthless picture roll that he had been instructed to burn a few weeks before. He told how Tari, Lesso, and Con had begged him not to burn it, but to let them have it. Now they were using it to teach those village boys the stories they had grown to love.

The mission lady was a good listener. She waited until he had finished the whole story, and then she said, "Kado, I, too, am happy. I know it is not your brothers who have been taking the things. This afternoon we discovered a group of mischievous monkeys taking the clothespins from the clothes on the line. We watched them, and noticed they were also helping themselves to any small articles they could find around the place. We drove them away; but they soon returned, bringing with them several things they had taken previously, dropping them down to us from the trees."

It was a happy Kado who went to sleep on his pallet that night. Before he closed his eyes he breathed a prayer of thankfulness: "Thank You, Lord, for my three good brothers."

KADO AND THE TWINS

K ADO," mother called, as she looked in the door of the humble home.

"Yes, mother," said Kado sleepily. He stretched slowly, gathered up the mat and blanket he had been sleeping on, put on his wrap-around garment, and sauntered out to wash and eat breakfast.

Kado was used to getting up at daylight, for there were many things to be done. Father and the three boys, Tari, Lesso, and Con, would go to the rice fields as usual. Kado and his mother would go to the woods with a group of villagers to get wood. They must not go alone, because there were rumors that a man-eating tiger had been seen in the hills.

Kado carried his hatchet to chop off the small branches. He helped mother tie the sticks into long bundles to carry on their heads. On the way home with the villagers, Kado overheard a conversation that made him sad. A young mother whom Kado knew had twin babies.

"It is too bad," said one of the women to Kado's mother. "How can twins live? There is hardly enough to feed one baby, but two! They will not live, I tell you. Already the one baby cries and cries. It is because the young mother has become a Christian. Trouble always comes when our people become Christians."

Kado's mother shifted the bundle of sticks she was carrying, but said nothing. She looked down at the thoughtful face of her son beside her.

"There must be some way to save the twins," said Kado's mother, as the other woman hurried away. "Surely it is not because the mother has become a Christian. Do you suppose the mission lady could do something to help her?"

"I'm sure she can," said Kado confidently. "I will go and ask her as soon as I take this bundle of wood home."

The mission lady listened sympathetically to Kado's account of the twins. "We will do what we can," she said. "Will you ask the young mother to bring her babies to the hospital at once? Perhaps we can find a way to help her."

"I will go right now," said Kado, his brown eyes sparkling with eagerness. He ran down the path toward that section of the village where the young mother lived.

At first the young woman refused to go. She had already been criticized for giving up her idol worship to become a Christian. Her neighbors had warned her that the babies would die because she had refused the weird incantations of the charm doctor.

Finally Kado persuaded the young mother to go with him to the mission hospital, assuring her that the mission doctor and his workers would do their best to save her babies. Tenderly Kado carried one baby, while the mother followed him, carrying the one who cried.

The mission lady was very kind. She prepared a formula using condensed milk, and showed the mother how to wash the bottles and keep the milk in a bowl of cold water so that ants would not get in.

The tiny babies eagerly drank the milk from the bottles. The one who had cried was soon satisfied and went to sleep. The mother looked at her babies lying on the clean white bed. She looked at Kado and then up at the mission lady. Tears of gratitude flowed down her cheeks as she tried to express her thanks.

"You are so good! How can I ever pay you for showing me how to feed my twin babies?"

For several days the young mother made frequent trips to the hospital to be sure the formula was right.

"You are learning fast," the mission lady assured her. "Now you should be able to prepare the formula at home. Do not be discouraged at what your neighbors say. Someday they, too, will see that it pays to be a Christian."

After a prayer for the young mother and the babies, the mission lady gave her a reassuring pat on the arm and sent her happily on her way.

"Come back again if you are not sure," invited the mission lady.

With a song in his heart, Kado turned to his work. Someday those tiny twins would be big enough to go to the mission school. Someday they, too, would sing the Jesus song.

The boys raced off across the yard as the doctor and his wife watched. "I want the boys to learn to take directions," the man declared.

WHY KADO AND TARI WON THE RACE

A RACE?" Kado looked at Tari with amazement. This was something different from the regular classwork. It would be exciting. The missionary often used strange methods to illustrate certain lessons. He believed in giving concrete examples whenever possible, and this was to be one of them.

"A race will be fun," said Tari, his brown eyes glistening with anticipation.

The missionary drew a line in the dust with a pointed stick. Then he gave each boy a small covered ball of cotton and white muslin, that the mission lady had prepared.

"Hold these in your right hand until you reach the spring," said the missionary. "Then transfer them to the left hand while you take a drink. After that put them back in your right hand. You will then run up the hill where there are three large rocks. Touch the center of the third rock with your ball, and return by the old buffalo path to the mail road and back to this spot. I will be waiting here by the big tree to welcome the winners. Do you understand the instructions?"

The group of boys answered Yes! They stood looking down at their brown toes on the line in the dust. In each right hand was a white cotton ball. They were eager to begin the race. The missionary counted, "One, two, three—GO!"

The boys were off across the lawn toward the spring. The mission lady smiled as she saw them go. She looked up at her husband and said, "You do think of the most interesting, practical, and impressive ways to teach them. What is it this time?"

"I want to show the boys that they must learn to take directions exactly," he replied. "While they drink from the spring, the right hand will become wet; that will moisten the muslin ball enough to pick up purple marks from the indelible pencil I rubbed on the third rock. If they go to the rock first, there will be no marks because the muslin balls will be dry. They must carry out instructions exactly in order to win this race. This race is not for speed, but accuracy."

With joyous shouts, the racers bounded across the lawn toward the spring, excited and eager to win the race. There would be no prize, but there would be the satisfaction of winning the race. A smile of approval from the kind face of the missionary was reward enough.

Kado and Tari were in the lead at first, but when the path grew narrow, some of the boys who were larger, pushed on ahead, leaving them at the end of the line. Each boy wanted to be the first to lay his little white ball at the feet of the missionary.

Some of the boys stooped to drink of the spring, while others ran on to the rocks without waiting for their turn at the spring.

Kado thought his turn to drink would never come. Some of the boys were already half way up the hill toward the three rocks.

"Let's not wait to drink," said Tari to Kado. "They are all so far ahead of us, we will never win now."

"But the missionary said—" Kado held his right hand under the cold stream of water and took one big swallow. "Hurry, Tari, we are the last ones."

Tari stooped and held his right hand and took a drink of cold water from the spring. Then he followed Kado up the hill toward the three rocks.

"Why do we have to go clear up there?" asked Tari. "The other boys are already on the buffalo trail. There is no use. They will beat us anyway; we are so far behind."

But Kado insisted, "The missionary said for us to touch the third rock, so I will do exactly as he said, even if I don't win the race." Tari followed Kado up the hill. The brothers touched the third rock, as they had been told to do.

"There is no need to run now," said Kado, "for they are all so far ahead of us. It has been fun anyway. At least we did exactly as we were told to do."

"Some of the boys did not even go up to the rocks," said Tari. "And some of them did not wait for a drink."

"We will not tell," said Kado loyally.

"No," said Tari, "we will not tell."

The missionary and his wife were waiting by the big tree for all the boys to return. When all the little white balls were placed in a row at their feet, they would announce the winners.

Quite out of breath, Kado and Tari came hurrying up, and placed their white muslin balls on the ground at the feet of the missionary. The boys looked on with interest as the missionary inspected the little white balls one by one. Then the missionary shook his head and said, "I can find only two boys who have carried out instructions fully—only two." He held up two of the white balls for all to see. "Do you see these little purple marks? These marks tell me that two of the boys took a drink at the spring, placed the little white ball in the right hand, then with the ball wet from their hand, they touched it to the center of the third rock on the hillside. This morning while I was taking my early morning stroll, I rubbed my magic pencil on the third rock only, so those who touched their ban to another rock, even though they were wet, did not pick up any purple marks. These two balls belong to Kado and Tari. They have won the race, as you can see."

The boys grew serious and looked up into the face of the missionary. They asked, "May we run again? We win do it right this time. We will do exactly as you tell us."

The missionary only smiled and said, "I think you have already learned your lesson today. It is the same in the race of life. Each of us runs in the race, but few win because they do not follow directions. What the God in heaven tells us to do we must do exactly. We cannot cut across, substitute, or miss. May our two winners, Kado and Tari, always be faithful in carrying out orders. May they always be winners in the race of life."

At the close of the lesson, Kado and Tari tucked their little white muslin balls inside the folds of their clothing. "I will keep mine with me," said Kado, "to remind me that it pays to do exactly as you are told. I want to do what the God in heaven tells me to do. I want to always be a winner."

"And so do I," said Tari.

KADO'S PRISONER

IT WAS not quite daylight, but already the little village was astir with activity. Boys with bundles of bedding and personal belongings were hurrying down the lanes to the main road where the oxcarts were waiting. Kado and his three brothers, Tari, Lesso, and Con, were excited as they hastened down the path that led across the mission schoolyard, for this was the day for which they had been waiting. Today they were going with the missionary and a group of students to spend ten wonderful days in the hills.

Perhaps if Kado lived in our country, he would call it Summer Camp. They would meet other missionaries and Christian boys, and together they would study and pray and sing.

"Hurry, Kado," called Tari, "they are all ready to start."

"I will be with you in just a moment," replied Kado, turning toward the mission house, where he saw a light in the study window. Kado would stop only a moment to say good-by to the mission lady and express his appreciation for the wonderful opportunity he had to go to the hills with Christian friends.

Not waiting for an answer to his timid knock, Kado opened the door, and stood in the dimly lighted study room. No one was there. He looked around at the familiar articles of furniture—the shelves filled with books, the couch, the easel with the drawing board, the kneehole desk, the wastebasket. Then his eyes shifted upward to the picture of Jesus which hung above the desk. Kado loved that picture, and he sought every opportunity to look into the kind eyes of the One the artist had pictured as the Saviour.

Suddenly, Kado sensed a movement under the desk, and by instinct he stepped back quickly. Curled up in the shadows of the square space beneath the desk was a deadly snake! Shivers of fear ran up and down the back of the boy's neck. His first impulse was to run. Then he realized that soon the mission lady would come into the room and seat herself at her usual place at the desk.

The oxcarts were ready to start; he must not keep them waiting. His roll of bedding was just outside the door. He should hurry and join his brothers. Yet—if he did not see the mission lady to warn her! Yes, he must do something.

There was a slight stirring under the desk. The snake peered up at him with beady eyes.

"If I could find something to put in front of the desk," said Kado to himself, "I would keep him in the little square space until help comes."

Seizing the large drawing board from the easel, he placed it lengthwise across the opening, and at the same time pushed the desk back against the wall, shutting the snake in as a prisoner. Then, with a prayer in his heart, Kado placed his trembling body firmly against the drawing board to hold it in place. His heart beat rapidly as he felt the writhing of his prisoner angrily lashing its wriggling body against the drawing board in a violent effort to escape. The boy continued to hold the drawing board in place even though the muscles of his arms and body ached. Seconds seemed like minutes, minutes seemed like hours, as he waited, tense and anxious for help to come.

Kado held the drawing boad over the hole in the desk front. His prisoners must not escape! As he waited he looked up at the picture of Jesus.

Then he heard the creaking of cart wheels. The oxcarts would soon be far up the road. He was left behind! Tears of bitter disappointment welled up in his eyes. He shifted his position and took a firmer hold on the drawing board. His prisoner must not escape! Through his tears he looked up at the picture above him—the Man of Sorrows. Kado became thoughtful. A memory verse came to his mind as he waited: "Greater love hath no man than this, that a man lay down his life for his friends." The mission lady was one of his friends. She had come with her husband to this country to tell his people of Jesus, who died to save them. She was giving her life in service for the Master. Yes, Kado would gladly give up his trip to the hills for her sake. That would be what Jesus would do, if He were here.

Somehow, while Kado was pondering about that love, the prisoner under the desk became more quiet; the violent thrashing ceased. Only a subdued movement could be felt against the drawing board.

"He must have decided he cannot escape," thought Kado. "How I wish I could have gone with the missionary to the hills. I am glad Tari, Lesso, and Con could go. They will tell me all about it when they return."

"Kado." A voice startled him. "Kado, what are you doing here?" It was the mission lady standing in the doorway, with a look of surprise on her face. "Why are you not with the boys?"

"Oh, please!" begged Kado, "call the men. Get help! There is a snake in here behind the drawing board!"

In a short time the mission lady returned with Tim and Orlo, armed with weapons. Cautiously they approached the desk and took away the drawing board. Kado stood beside the mission lady at a safe distance.

"There is no need to strike it," said Tim. "It is dead already. See, Kado, you crushed his head when you pushed the desk back against the wall."

"Thank you, Kado," said the mission lady as she watched Tim carry the limp body of the snake away. "Although a 'Thank you' cannot express my real feelings for the risk you took to save me. Perhaps you'd better hurry down to the road now. They are waiting for you."

"The oxcarts? Waiting for me? Didn't they go?"

Hastily picking up his bedroll, Kado ran a few steps down the path. Suddenly he turned and came back, and shyly said, "I came back to tell you 'Thank you.' Good-by. And please watch for dangers." In another moment Kado was far down the road, anticipating a wonderful time in the hills.

The mission lady shaded her eyes against the rising sun as she watched the oxcarts disappear around the bend. Then she turned back into the study room with a prayer of thankfulness in her heart, thankful that the "greater love" had also come into Kado's heart.

A GIFT FOR KADO

THE oxcarts creaked slowly along the dusty road, one behind the other. Within the carts were supplies, rolls of bedding, and the missionary with his group of happy boys. Over and over they sang their favorite songs as they rode along. Now and then they stopped to let the oxen drink from a stream or munch tufts of grass by the roadside. During these intervals the boys crawled out of the carts to rest their cramped legs. Sometimes they ran along the road to examine a flower or tree. The missionary was interested in things of nature, and he drew spiritual lessons from them for the boys.

Kado and his brothers were always interested. This was a new experience to them, and they enjoyed every moment of the trip. It was evening when they reached the end of the journey. A campfire was burning in the center of an enclosure, which was surrounded by newly built houses and a large meeting place. Around the fire was a group of boys who greeted the newcomers in a friendly manner. There were also native workers and two missionaries who seemed to know exactly what to do and say to make the visitors feel at ease. The oxen were cared for, and the boys were given supper. Then they all gathered around the fire to sing and to listen to the stories that never grow old. Kado and the boys were assigned to their places for the night; and before they realized it, the signal had been given for all to be quiet.

"Tari," whispered Kado from the pallet, "isn't this wonderful?"

"Yes," Tari whispered back. "I'm glad we could come. Do you suppose heaven will be like this?"

"It will be even better," said Kado, "because there will be nothing in heaven to be afraid of—no dangers, no sin. Tari, do you know what I want?"

"No," answered Tari. "What?"

Kado was in earnest as he whispered. "I want one of those books such as the missionaries have that tell about Jesus and heaven. I know I could learn to read it. Do you think if I prayed for a book like that—"

"Oh, Kado," said Tari, "they cost many rupees. Only the missionaries can have those books. Better go to sleep and forget it."

Kado was silent. Yes, those books would cost many rupees; but it might be a good idea to pray about it anyway. The mission lady back home said that if we ask in His name, believing, we will receive. Kado believed that nothing is impossible with God and that it is only our lack of faith and our failure to ask that keeps us from receiving the blessings God is waiting to give.

"—Just a Bible, one that I can read. Teach me what it means, and I will follow what it says to do. Amen."

All was silent in the little room. Tari and Kado were soon fast asleep, for they were tired from their long ride. Their bodies needed rest, for tomorrow would be filled with new, exciting activities.

The ten days passed all too quickly. Kado and his three brothers enjoyed every moment, from the sound of the drums in the early morning to the "All quiet" signal after the campfire at night. Exercise, races, handcraft, the story hour, wholesome food at regular intervals—everything helped to make the camp a success. At the end of the ten days several of the boys expressed their desire to be baptized, among whom were Tari, Kado, Lesso, and Con.

Again the oxcarts rumbled along the dusty road, loaded with boys with happy faces. Again songs echoed through the valleys and across the lotus pools and paddy fields.

It was a happy home-coming. The mission lady was waiting, her face beaming with pleasure as she welcomed back her husband and his group of boys.

"And Kado!" she said, patting his brown shoulder, "I have something for you. Come with me." She led the way to the study room and gave the boy a small package, which he opened eagerly.

"For me?" he asked, as he unwrapped a copy of the Bible in his own language, Telugu.

"Yes, Kado, it was sent here to be given to someone who will appreciate it. I thought of you. Would you like to have it?"

Kado looked at the volume in his hand and then at the mission lady. "Did God send this to me? He must have, because I prayed for it, as you told us to pray, believing. But I did not think He would send it so soon. Of course I like it. I want to learn to read it. Someday I will be a missionary and tell people about the God in heaven who gives wonderful gifts to us."

Kado was proud to show his precious gift to his brothers and his parents. Day by day one could see the boy studying the strange characters that look like hooks and eyes. Kado was learning fast, and whenever he had a chance he would read aloud to his parents and his brothers.

"It is not in vain," said the mission lady to her husband. "We surely chose the right one when we decided that we should give the Bible to Kado."

KADO FINDS LOTUS BUD

S LOWLY, steadily the two oxen pulled the crude plow through the field. Kado followed behind his father as he guided the plow. Kado's work was to pull away the broken tree roots that were plowed up, and pile them along the path to be taken home later for fuel. The day was warm, and both father and Kado wore but little clothing. Their brown backs were shining with streams of perspiration as they worked.

"Go on," father urged the tired oxen. Kado watched them plod down the rugged furrow until they disappeared around the hill. Then he bent to the task of lifting a large gnarled root from its bed of upturned soil. As he laid it on the pile at the side of the strip of plowing, he thought he heard a strange cry, which seemed to come from the valley below.

"An animal," said Kado to himself, as he peered into the dark shadows among the trees across the valley. Seeing nothing, he continued piling up the scattered roots.

Then he heard it again. This time he knew it was not the cry of an animal. It was a human cry—a cry of distress.

Down at the foot of the hill was a narrow pole bridge that crossed the stream. On the opposite side of the bridge was a woman holding a small baby in her arms. The call came again, very distinctly this time. "Help me, boy. I need someone, quickly."

The woman held a baby. "Help me, boy," she said. "My husband is dead. I, too, will die, and there is no one to care for little Lotus Bud."

Without a moment's hesitation Kado ran down into the valley and across the bridge.

"Help me, boy," she repeated. "My husband is dead. I, too, will die, and there is no one to care for my precious Lotus Bud. The charm doctor did not help; he could not cure the fever. Will you take her to the missionary for me? I am so weak I cannot carry her farther. Take her to the missionary. I will lie down under a tree. There I can die in peace, knowing you will find someone to care for my Lotus Bud."

Kado stood at the end of the pole bridge. He could see the marks of illness in the woman's face. He realized the danger from contact with one who had fever; but she was one of God's children, one whom the missionary had come to help. She needed medical care, but she was too weak to go on. He could carry the baby to the treatment room and bring help for the mother.

Kado knew that the missionary would do what he could. He had watched the workers bring in patients to the treatment room, some with fever, some with sores, some with terrible marks from animal claws. The missionary had helped them. Surely he would help the mother of little Lotus Bud.

With a bit of misgiving, Kado took the baby in his arms and said: "I will carry her to the missionary; then I will come back with help for you. Rest there under the tree, but please don't die. Wait until the missionary has a chance to help you."

Kado carried the child across the pole bridge and up the hill toward the mission house. The baby cried softly; her body felt unusually warm through the shawl in which she was wrapped.

"I must hurry," said Kado, as he climbed the hill and followed the furrow to the end of the field. There he met his father with the oxen.

"What have you there, Kado?" he asked.

"It is Lotus Bud. I found her down in the valley across the bridge. I am taking her to the missionary. She is sick with fever. Her mother is sick, too. I will help with the roots as soon as I take her to the missionary and get help for the mother. I will hurry."

The mission lady was kind and sympathetic. She took the baby from Kado's tired arms and placed her on the resting couch. She instructed Kado to wash carefully, using a disinfecting solution. She summoned Tim and Orlo to take a stretcher and go with Kado to bring the sick mother to the hospital. Then she turned her attention to Lotus Bud. First, she bathed the small, fevered body and put on clean clothing. The missionary doctor was called in to give the baby medical care. Soon the crying had ceased, and Lotus Bud was asleep in a clean, white crib sheet.

In a little while Kado and the two workers entered the room with the baby's mother. As they placed her gently on the bed, she opened her eyes and asked, "Where is my Lotus Bud? My sick baby."

Tenderly the mission lady stroked the hot forehead and whispered, "She is asleep in the next room. She will soon be all right. But now we are going to help you."

Kado followed the native boys out of the room, leaving the mission lady and her helpers to do what they could for the mother.

As Kado returned to his work in the field with his father, he prayed that God would take away the fever, so that Lotus Bud and her mother might learn to love Jesus. He knew that the missionary, the mission lady, and the native nurses were praying, too, and that they would make the patients as comfortable as was humanly possible.

While Kado was thinking of the sick ones, the missionary and his group of helpers ministered to the needs of the sick mother; then they gathered in the office to pray. The missionary wiped the perspiration from his forehead and said, "Why do they wait so long before coming to us? The treatments of the charm doctors have only added to the seriousness of the case. We have done all we can. We will leave the rest in the hands of the Great Physician."

For many days the mother lay on the white bed, growing weaker and weaker. She did not hear the lusty cries of Lotus Bud. The missionary worked and prayed earnestly. The death of an unbelieving native would only mean added prejudice among the people.

Kado noticed the sadness on the face of the mission lady as he saw her from time to time. Was she worried about the mother of little Lotus Bud? The fever had claimed so many victims. He also knew what it would mean to the missionary and his wife if the woman should die. It would make it harder to build up the confidence of the people, and the good work would be hindered.

That evening after supper, Kado gathered his family for worship. His father, mother, and three brothers joined in one petition: "If it be God's will, may the life of the mother of little Lotus Bud be spared so that she can go back to her people and tell them of the love of Jesus."

Kado had faith, and all his family believed, too. That night as Kado lay on his pallet in the corner of the hut, he continued to pray. Early in the morning Kado hurried to the mission house to play with Lotus Bud. She was quite well now, and would laugh and clap her hands, and wiggle her brown toes when she saw Kado coming to amuse her.

The mission lady met him at the door. She was smiling, and a new light seemed to gleam in her eyes, as she said, "I have good news for you this morning, Kado. Lotus Bud's mother is much better. The fever is gone, and she is sitting up on the bed, eating! Lotus Bud is sitting on the bed beside her, laughing and playing. Come and see, Kado. We are so happy. The Lord has answered our prayers."

The mother beamed when she saw Kado. She thanked him over and over for taking Lotus Bud to the missionary. The woman cried as she clasped her baby, and she said, "I will stay until I am well. I want to learn more about the Great Doctor who made my precious Lotus Bud well. He is making me well, too. He took the fever away. The missionary is good. Everybody who loves

Jesus is good. I want to love Him, too, and tell my people about the God in heaven who makes people well."

Once more Kado piled the gnarled tree roots beside the path as the oxen slowly pulled the crude plow over the field. Now and then he looked at the pole bridge across the stream in the valley. Little Lotus Bud and her mother had gone back over the bridge to their home. They were no longer burning with fever, for the Great Physician had given them new strength and a new hope.

No more would the charm doctor be called for little Lotus Bud. In the future she would be taken to the missionary if she needed medical care. She would be lulled to sleep, not by the weird chanting of the devil worshipers, but by the Jesus song Kado and the mission lady had taught the mother to sing.

Kado lifted a large root to the top of the pile, then stood for a moment with closed eyes and bowed head.

He said, "Thank You, God, for helping me find Lotus Bud."

KADO AND THE SADHU

IT WAS a busy day for Kado. In the early morning, even before the sun peeped over the jungle trees, Kado and his parents and his three brothers were out in the rice fields. There was much work to be done, for the small paddy plants must be transplanted from the seedbeds. They must be taken up and set out in the larger field, where they would not be so crowded. The fields were flooded from the summer rains, and ridges of earth, bunds, must be built around the fields to keep the water in. Since these fields were on the hillside, they must be terraced. This meant hard work for the entire family.

Kado and his three brothers knew what it meant to work. The day was warm, and the task of transplanting the paddy plants seemed endless. They were glad when the sun was overhead, for then they could sit in a shady place to eat and rest. They were thankful for the cooked rice in their gourds. All too soon the work began again.

"I never saw so many paddy plants before in all my life," sighed Tari, as the shadows of the afternoon began to lengthen. "I am beginning to think that workdays are the longest days."

"But think of all the good rice we will have when the harvest is over and when it is schooltime again," said Kado to his brother.

The boys were looking forward to the opening of school. They had learned many things at the mission school. They looked down the hill at the village, nestled in the valley. That was "home, sweet home" to them. There were the mission buildings with the red-tiled roofs. They saw the river and the pond, where the big, long-horned water buffaloes were lying in the water to keep cool, while village boys played nearby. Farther up the river, women were washing clothes, rubbing them on stones on the riverbank. In a pasture a small boy was watching the animals that grazed on the sparse grass. With a stick in his right hand, and his baby sister hanging on his left hip, cradled in a strip of cloth, the boy strolled along, keeping his eyes on the cattle.

"It will soon be suppertime," said Kado. "The sun is sinking low. If we hurry we can finish this field before dark."

Kado and Tari bent to the task, and soon father called them. He was ready to go home. Picking up their empty gourd shells, they started down the path toward home. The family gathered around the bowl of rice and lentils; but before they began to eat, Con announced that a visitor was coming toward the house.

"It is the sadhu," whispered Lesso, as father arose to welcome him.

Mother expressed her welcome by placing a flat dish of rice before the sadnu, in order to include him in the family circle around the rice bowl.

A sadhu is a wandering preacher who travels about carrying a blanket, depending upon the hospitality of the people for his food and shelter.

After supper they sat around a campfire, listening to the stories of the outside world as told by the sadhu. Kado listened eagerly as the man told of his travels through dangerous country, and of his escapes from wild animals and hostile tribes. He told many incidents which proved God's protecting care.

"The Lord is good to us," said the sadhu reverently, as he took a small stringed instrument from the folds of his blanket. Kado and the boys gathered around to examine the instrument. It was a simple, homemade affair, with wires stretched over a half cocoanut shell to a stick fastened in the end. A little bridge was inserted over the strings, and there it was—a crude violin!

Drawing a bow over the strings, the sadhu played a few uncertain notes. Then he began to play a familiar hymn. Kado and Tari hummed as he played. The sadhu concluded the hymn and began feeling along the strings, trying to think of another.

"Can you play the Jesus song?" asked Kado timidly.

"Is this the one?" asked the sadhu, playing a bit uncertainly.

"N—no," said Lesso, "it's not that tune."

The sadhu invited the boys to sing it for him. He soon learned the tune and played it while they sang. Father, Lesso, and Con joined the singing, and the sadhu seemed happy that everyone was having a good time.

Soon the fire dwindled to a bed of red embers. The family spread blankets on the mud floor and were soon fast asleep.

The man in the bushes arose to show the boys his deep wounds where the bear had clawed him. The boys took the injured man to the mission.

KADO AND TIM

THE bund is out! The bund is out!" cried Con, running swiftly toward the house. Kado, Lesso, and Tari told father, and they soon hurried out to build up the mud-and-stone wall that kept the water in the paddy fields.

"It broke in only one place," said Con, as they hurried along the path. When they arrived at the spot they could see that some animal had run through the field during the night and loosened a rock that had rolled down on the terrace.

"It was a bear," said a voice from the bushes on the slope of the hill. "He is a mean bear, too." The man who was speaking arose to show where the animal had clawed him on his arm and back,

"You should go to the hospital at once," said Kado, knowing how important it is to care for such wounds immediately.

"But I can't go; it hurts too much. It is too far to the hospital; I would rather lie here in the shade."

"I will get Orlo and Tim to help me," said Kado. "We will take you to the missionary doctor."

While father and the boys repaired the mud wall, Kado ran to the hospital and returned with Tim and Orlo and the stretcher. Gently they placed the wounded man on the blanket and carefully they carried him to the treatment room, where the doctor was waiting. Kado stood in the doorway and watched the doctor as he cleansed the wounds and administered an anesthetic with his magic needle. Then the wounds were closed by stitches, and healing ointment and bandages were applied. When the doctor had finished, Tim and Orlo moved the patient to a bed, and Kado went back to help in the paddy fields.

That evening Kado went to the hospital again to see how the patient was. Tim said the man was sleeping quietly.

"You are a good helper, Tim," said Kado. "I don't know what the missionary would do without you and Orlo."

"He will soon find out," said Tim, "for I am leaving the mission soon."

"Leaving?" echoed Kado. "Where are you going?"

"To the city," said Tim, lowering his voice so that people passing would not hear him. "I am going to work in the big city. I am not happy with this kind of life. I want to earn lots of money. The rich people in the city pay big wages to boys to drive their automobiles. I know I could learn to drive an automobile. Just wait until I come back a rich man! I will show you a lot of things. No more oxcarts for me!"

"Oh, Tim," sighed Kado, "they need you here! You can do so much good helping the missionary. What about your schoolwork? Will you give that up, too?"

"There is plenty of time for book learning," said Tim. "At present I want some money."

As Tim turned back to his work, Kado asked, "When will you be leaving, Tim?"

"Soon, maybe tomorrow," he replied, and he disappeared around the corner of the corridor.

As Kado walked slowly home, he thought of his friend. He remembered it was Tim who had come to take away the poisonous snake that Kado had discovered in the study at the mission house. It was Tim who had helped to bring many patients, including the mother of little Lotus Bud, to the hospital for treatments. Tim was a brave boy. He was not afraid to face dangers when doing good deeds for others. Things would not be the same at the mission without Tim.

But perhaps Tim would be able to do even more good in the city. There were so many more people there who needed to know about Jesus. Perhaps Tim would have an opportunity to let his light shine to the rich people. As he rode along in a shiny big automobile he could sing the Jesus song. Maybe with the big wages he would receive he would help the mission school and hospital to buy medicines, books, and hospital equipment.

That night as Kado lay on his mat, he wished that he might go to the city with Tim. "How much good I could do with a lot of money!" he thought. "I know I have many things to learn right here at the mission, before I go out into the world. I will be content to stay here. until I am as old as Tim. Someday, perhaps I, too, may go to the big city and earn big wages with Tim."

KADO WATCHES THE RICE FIELDS

IT WAS harvest time, and Kado and several of the boys of the village were preparing to watch the fields during the night. They would frighten away the monkeys who raided the fields of ripe grain at night, destroying much of the crop by racing around and tearing up the plants.

The boys built small campfires and put up makeshift tents along the edge of the field. They took turns sleeping and watching. When a band of monkeys was heard approaching, the boys blew strong blasts on their crude horns. The noise would frighten away the monkeys for a time.

Kado was excited tonight as the boys prepared their camp and built up the fire. He was to watch with Tim and Orlo, and he knew that Tim would have many interesting things to tell of his life in the big city. Kado had missed Tim while he was away. How often he, too, had wished to go to the city to see the sights. Tim seemed quite well-to-do now, for he had good clothes, and had brought gifts to his parents and to the hospital staff. He had given Kado a new wrap-around garment and a knife with which to cut tree branches.

As the boys seated themselves on the ground, Tim was silent for several moments. Then he said, "Kado, you seem to be happy here, just as you were before I left. Are you really satisfied?"

"Oh, yes, Tim; I love it here at the mission. Don't you sometimes wish that you were still here, working for the missionary and the people who need you? Can you do a greater work for God in the big city among the rich people? You may have greater opportunity to let your light shine among so many."

Tim did not say a word. He only looked at Kado. Then he smiled a queer smile, and said, "Kado, I am different now. You think I am good as I tried to be when I worked for the missionary; but I have changed. Since I've been working in the city I've grown up. It is all right for you or Tari and Orlo to believe the Bible; it sounds nice when you hear it read, but it is not for me. I really don't care for it any more. I live differently now. I like to smoke and gamble."

Kado was shocked and hurt. Tim had been his hero, his ideal; and now, what had the big city done to him?

Suddenly a chattering noise was heard in the rustling bushes behind them. Instantly the watchers blew on their horns to frighten the monkeys back into the woods.

Soon it was Orlo and Tari's turn to watch, so Tim and Kado lay down in the tent to sleep. But Kado did not sleep. How could he sleep when his heart was troubled for his friend on the mat beside him?

"Money is a nice thing to have," decided Kado; "but it isn't everything. It can keep one from loving Jesus. It can keep one from entering heaven." A memory verse came into Kado's mind, "Seek ye first the kingdom of God, and His righteousness; and all these things shall be added unto you."

This verse had a real meaning for Kado. He knew that Tim was not really happy in his new life in the big city.

Somehow he must help his friend to realize that adventure and big wages do not bring happiness in themselves. Folding his hands, Kado prayed for his friend Tim.

Tim turned over on the mat. Evidently Tim was not asleep either,

"Tim," whispered Kado, "are you awake?"

"Yes," answered Tim. "I thought you were asleep, you were so still."

"Tim, are you really happy in the big city? Are you happy when you do things you know are not pleasing to God?"

"Well," Tim hesitated, "sometimes I think I am when I am out with the boys for a good time. It is really lots of fun while it lasts; but I would never advise you to try it, Kado. You are a good boy. I hope you will always work for God. Many times I have been lonesome for the hospital, and for all the good people here at the mission. I have been lonesome for you, too, Kado. Sometimes I even get lonesome for God!"

There was silence for a few moments. "Tim," said Kado, "won't you come back to God and live for Him? You will never be happy until you do. Tell God you are sorry you went away. He will forgive you. He loves you and will take you back. It says so in the Bible. Please, Tim."

There was a long silence. Kado prayed again. Then he asked, "Will you come back and live for God, Tim?"

"I will think about it, Kado; really I will."

Just then Orlo and Tari blew their horns. The monkeys had returned. Kado and Tim joined them to drive the monkeys out of the rice field.

As Kado and Tim sat again around the campfire, Kado asked, "Are you thinking, Tim?"

"Yes, Kado, I am thinking. Do you suppose the missionary would let me go back to school and work for the hospital again? I am not going back to the city."

"Do you really mean it, Tim? If you come back to God it will make everyone happy."

"Yes, Kado; after all, life in the city may be filled with adventure and lots of money. But what good are they when you get lonesome for God? I will stay."

Kado sat gazing into the fire. The crickets and beetles broke the stillness of the night with their strange sounds. Kado looked at his friend Tim sitting beside him, also gazing thoughtfully into the fire. "Thank You, God, for bringing Tim back," Kado whispered.

KADO AND THE CHARM DOCTOR

KADO went down the path toward the spring, carrying an earthen jar to be filled with water. This was cleaning day at the mission house, and Kado's job was to scrub the kitchen floor. Kado took pride in his work, and it helped pay expenses to go to school.

As Kado passed the hospital, he saw Tari, Lesso, and Con taking turns cutting grass with a curved sickle. They were earning their school money by keeping the grass cut and the bushes trimmed. Perhaps someday they would earn enough extra money to buy a Bible like the one Kado had received.

Kado called a cheery greeting to his brothers as he went down the path to the spring. Dipping his waterpot into the tank, the youth watched the ripples for a moment. Then he lifted the dripping jar to his shoulder and started back toward the mission house.

Suddenly a tall figure loomed up in the path before him. Kado's heart gave a leap, for in front of him stood the one man who had become an enemy of Kado's family since they had given up their idols and devil worship. He was the one man Kado feared—the charm doctor. Kado did not look at the familiar charms and gadgets hanging around his neck, arms, and waist; he saw only the evil look in those dark eyes scowling under black eyebrows. Those eyes came nearer and nearer. Kado shrank back a few steps as the charm doctor advanced, shaking his chain of bones, beetles, and shells.

Kado saw the evil look in the eyes of the charm doctor. The boy shrank back a few steps as the man advanced, shaking the bones and shells.

"You—you—" he said, pointing accusingly to Kado, "you are the cause of your father's leaving me. He and many others no longer pay me for my charms. Because you have influenced them to go to the mission you will receive the curse of the gods." He reached out his thin pointed finger and touched the jar of water, muttering between closed teeth, "Whoever drinks water from this jar will die."

Shaking his string of charms, he went on his way, chanting his weird tune. As he went up the hill, Kado stepped back into the path. He was tempted to throw the cursed water jug on the rocks and break it to bits, but it was not his jar. It belonged to the mission lady. And the water—why, the water would not be used for drinking purposes anyway; it was for scrubbing the kitchen floor. No one would drink from it, so the curse of the charm doctor would not work after all.

But what was that rumor he had heard about the baby who had died in the village? It was whispered that the charm doctor had put a curse on him because his parents had become Christians. It took courage and faith to stand against this superstition. Kado shuddered as he set the jar of water on the kitchen floor. The mission lady smiled as she usually did when Kado came to work for her, but her smile quickly turned to a look of anxiety as she saw the queer expression on Kado's face this morning. Something was wrong.

Kado did not sing at his work as he usually did; and kept looking over his shoulder in a frightened manner, as though he expected someone to slip up behind him to hurt him.

When the task was completed, Kado poured out the remaining water, turned the jar upside down in its usual corner, and covered it with the cleaning cloth. Then he went to the basin to wash. Taking a cake of soap from the folds of his garment, he carefully washed his hands. Not knowing exactly the difference between the curses of the charm doctor and germs, Kado thought perhaps the soap would wash away the curse if he rubbed hard enough.

Once when an epidemic of the dreaded fever had threatened their village, the mission lady had cut a bar of soap into four parts and had given the pieces to Kado and his three brothers. These bits of soap were treasures to the boys, for to them soap had been an unknown article. The mission lady instructed them how to boil their drinking water, and how to keep their faces and hands free from germs. "If that little cake of soap kills germs," Kado had said, "I will carry it with me wherever I go."

Now as he washed his hands vigorously, he hoped to wash away the curse of the charm doctor as well as the germs.

"Is something troubling you, Kado?" asked the mission lady kindly. At first Kado feared to tell her, lest the curse come upon her, too. But finally he yielded to her questions and told her what had happened.

The mission lady soon calmed his fears, and after prayer together, Kado went home, the burden lifted from his heart.

The family gathered around their bowl of rice and beans that mother had prepared for the evening meal. It had been a busy day for everyone. The boys had finished cutting the grass by the hospital. Father and mother had been cultivating and hoeing in the field. Everyone was tired, and soon each one spread his blankets on the floor and prepared for sleep. Kado tried to sleep, but in the darkness his thoughts troubled him in spite of the comforting words of the mission lady. Small doubts kept creeping into his mind.

Suddenly there was a disturbance in the enclosure where the animals were kept. A calf bawled; the mother cow answered. There were strange rustling sounds in the bushes. Kado listened. He sat up on his pallet and tried to look through the darkness to see what was happening. Could it be that a leopard had come down from the hills to steal a calf?

In a moment the whole family was awake. Father and the four boys, armed with clubs and sticks, went out to the enclosure. Yes, the new calf was gone. The spotted leopard had disappeared in the tangled undergrowth, taking the calf with him. Father was silent; he did not scold as he had on a previous occasion.

Kado knew that many times trials come to those who choose to worship the God in heaven. This was one of those trials. Earnestly he prayed that no further trouble would come to them. He felt sure that his father would not be influenced by the charm doctor to go back to the worship of monkeys and devil gods. Kado's father had faith; he believed in the God in heaven.

When morning came, Kado went with his father to the fields. Father did not seem to mind the loss of the calf. He was happy, singing at his work.

"Thank You, God," Kado whispered. "Thank You for making us strong. Help us always to be true in spite of the curses of the charm doctor."

KADO, ORLO, AND THE WILD MAN

ONE bright morning, Kado and Orlo were walking through the woods. Birds were singing in the treetops overhead; monkeys were chattering among the branches, scampering noisily away as the boys approached. Parrots and peacocks screamed as they hurried to a place of safety, and shy little rabbits scurried under bushes.

Kado and Orlo were not out in the woods to hunt or to molest the wild things of the forest. They had come to gather material for their handcraft class. Long, slender vines were needed to complete the basket weaving. The vines were green when gathered, but they turned to a deep maroon when they were dry. They added color to the baskets, making them attractive to sell.

"There are some over there," said Kado, pointing to a cluster of tall trees from which hung long, slender streamers.

"Careful, now," warned Orlo, "there may be—"

Kado knew. Snakes were everywhere. One must be always on the alert. The boys gathered vines until they thought they had enough. They tied them in a bundle with a strip of muslin that Orlo carried around his waist.

As they started home, Orlo suggested, "Why not take a short cut through this valley?" "All right," said Kado, leading the way down a narrow path into the valley. "It will be shorter this way."

The path ended abruptly, turning at right angles to the left. In front of them, well-hidden from the path, was a tumble-down cabin. The thatch of the roof was partly gone, and most of one wall was missing.

"I guess nobody lives here," said Kado, looking in the door.

Suddenly Orlo screamed. From out of nowhere, it seemed, an arrow came flying through the air, hitting Orlo on the arm, piercing the flesh below the shoulder.

"Oh!" cried Orlo. "Get down Kado, quick! Someone is shooting at us. Look, an arrow—right in my arm!"

Kado turned to look. Then he heard, "Thief, thief! Get out of there!"

From out of the bushes came a man, hobbling along with the aid of a stick. He was waving his bow in the air, screaming, "Thief, thief! I caught you this time!"

His hair was shaggy and tousled; his eyes were wild and glaring. His garment, what was left of it, was ragged and dirty.

"It's the wild man," said Kado, as the old man limped toward the cabin. Kado and Orlo stood still. They must explain to him that they were not stealing, that they had only stopped to look.

"What are you doing here?" screamed the old man. "Stealing my honey again? Well, I have caught you this time."

"We did not steal your honey," said Orlo, trying to remove the sharp arrow from his arm.

"Please believe us," said Kado. "We do not steal. We meant no harm. We were gathering vines up on the hill, and were going home the short way through the valley. We did not know this was your home."

"It is not my home," said the old man. His voice was more subdued. "I am a poor man. I live on the hillside with my wife, my daughter, and my little grandson,

Addu. I gather wild honey to sell for a living. But right now there is not much sale for it, so I keep it stored in this old cabin. But somebody has been stealing it from me. I said I would shoot the first person I saw around this cabin."

Orlo was trying to remove the arrow from his arm. Kado was doing what he could to help, but it was deeply imbedded in the flesh.

"Take my knife, Kado," said Orlo. "Cut right here."

"No, no!" screamed the man. "Do not cut the flesh. It is bad luck."

"But we must," insisted Orlo, "in order to get the arrow out."

"I hate to do this," began Kado, "not because of superstition, but because it will make a bigger wound. It will hurt you, Orlo; but it has to be done."

Kado did as he was told, though his hand trembled. The wild man looked on, silently shaking his head. He admired the calm, brave manner of these two boys, who seemed to know what to do. He was sorry, now, that he had been hasty to shoot before finding out for sure that they were the thieves. He leaned heavily on his stick and kept saying over and over, "I'm sorry, I'm sorry. You are good boys. I am sorry."

Finally the arrow was out. Kado bandaged the bleeding arm with the strip of muslin from around the bundle of vines.

"Now we must hurry back to the mission," said Kado. "We must lose no time. That arm must be treated right away."

"The mission!" screamed the old man; "don't go to the mission! Don't you know they are Christians?"

"Yes, we know they are Christians, for, you see, we are Christians, too," said Kado. "We belong to the mission. We worship the God in heaven; we go to the mission school. Orlo works at the mission hospital. The missionary doctor will take good care of his arm. He will use his magic needle and take away the germs with magic water. He is very kind, and the mission lady is kind, too."

Then a sudden thought came to Kado's mind. He said, "Why don't you go to the mission lady to sell your honey? I know she does not have any right now, and I am sure she would buy some."

The old man had a puzzled expression on his face. He was anxious to sell his honey, but could he go to the mission to sell it?

Kado and Orlo started to leave, but the old man held Kado a moment by the arm. "Do you really think the mission lady would buy my honey?" he asked. He was trembling from head to foot, for he realized that he had spoken to Christians.

"Yes, I am quite sure," said Kado. "She was asking me just yesterday if I knew anyone who had honey to sell. Nobody has brought any to the mission house for a long time. But we must go now. That arm must be treated by the missionary right away."

It seemed a long way back to the mission. The sun was hot overhead. Orlo felt weak and dizzy at times, and his arm pained severely.

"Just pray, Orlo, that we may get back to the mission before you faint. I am sure I could not carry you," said Kado.

With the bundle of vines under one arm, and Orlo leaning on the other, Kado went slowly down the path toward the mission hospital. Quickly the missionary doctor treated Orlo's arm and put him to bed to rest.

"It will be all right in a few days," he told the boys. Kado stayed with Orlo until he went to sleep, then he went back to his weaving.

The shaggy-haired man leaned on a stick, and across his shoulders he carried a long pole, from each end of which hung large earthen jars.

The next afternoon a strange figure was seen coming up the path toward the mission house. It was an old man with shaggy hair, wearing a clean, though ragged, garment. He was leaning heavily upon a stick. Across his shoulders he carried a pole and from each end hung a large earthen jar. In his free hand he had a parcel. He came and stood before the door of the mission house.

The mission lady came to the door to greet the visitor in her usual friendly manner.

"I came to see the boy," he said in a low voice, "the boy I shot with my arrow. Is he here?"

"He is at the mission hospital, right over there," she said, pointing the direction.

"You, you are the mission lady?" he asked.

She nodded and smiled.

"I brought you some honey," he said, resting his burden on the path. "I understand you can use some. I do not want any pay for this. I am going to give it to you to pay for medicine and treatments for the boy's arm. I am sorry I shot him. He is a good boy. He did not steal my honey. It was a bear that was the thief. I caught him in my cabin last night. He will not steal my honey any more."

The old man untied the earthen jars from the pole. They were quite heavy, filled with honey, and sealed at the top with beeswax. In the parcel was more honey, still in the comb.

"It is all for you if you can use it," he said. "And now may I go to see the boy?"

The mission lady thanked the old man, and she went with him to the hospital to see Orlo. The old man held Orlo's hand and then sobbed. "Forgive me, please forgive me," he said sincerely.

"Yes, of course," said Orlo. "You see, my arm is going to be all right. The missionary doctor took good care of it with the magic needle and magic water, and the God in heaven will make it heal."

"The God in heaven—" repeated the old man. "My little grandson Addu talks about the God in heaven. He wants to come to the evening meetings at the mission to learn about the God in heaven. He has begged many times to go. Some of the boys at the school have told him stories, and he wants to learn more."

"We would be glad to have your grandson come," said the mission lady. "And you, too," she added. She thanked the man again for the honey. "And if you have any more honey when this is gone, I will be glad to pay you for it. We use a great deal of honey here at the mission."

"I will come back," said the old man. "I will come back."

KADO SINGS FOR ADDU

ONE morning as Kado was returning from the spring with a jar of fresh water, he heard someone calling, "Kado, Kado, wait!"

Kado lowered the jar of water from his shoulder and stood still. The old man who sold honey came unsteadily down the path, leaning on his stick.

"Good morning, grandpa," Kado greeted. "Are you out so early enjoying this lovely day?"

The man addressed as grandpa did not seem interested in the day, for he said, "It is Addu, my little grandson, Addu—he has had an accident. About a week ago he was picking fruit in a tree, and the branch he was leaning against broke, and he fell."

"Did he get hurt, grandpa?" asked Kado.

"Well, he must have broken his arm; it is all puffed up, and he says there are sharp pains in it. He keeps calling for you, Kado. He wants you to come to him. He says you are his friend."

"Of course, I will go to him, grandpa. Wait here for me, while I take this water to the mission house. Then I will go with you to see Addu."

Lifting the water jar to his shoulder again, Kado hurried down the path to the mission house. He explained what had happened, and then he hurried out the door. "If we can help him, let us know, Kado," she called after him.

"Yes, ma'am," said Kado, and he ran to join grandpa.

Following the trail through bushes, making their way across fields of rice and pasture land, Kado and the old grandfather came at last to the rude hut where Addu lived. The grandmother and Addu's mother were wringing their hands and chanting the weird song of the charm doctor. They arose from the floor when Kado and grandpa came in.

"Oh, Kado," said the mother, "our little Addu is very sick. He has fever, he cannot eat. We have done all that we can do. The charm doctor does not help him. We have rubbed cow manure on his arm for eight days, and he is no better. He only becomes worse."

"If you had taken him to the mission right away," said Kado, "I am sure the kind missionary and the mission lady could have helped him. They do not use cow manure on broken arms. They have a magic needle that makes the pain go away. They wash the sores with magic water that keeps all the germs out. But best of all, they pray to the God in heaven, and He is the One who makes the patients well. It is not too late. Shall I go for Tim and Orlo to bring Addu to the mission hospital on the stretcher? Is that the best thing to do?"

"No, he cannot be moved," said the grandmother firmly. "It would not be wise to move him now. He is very weak."

"Perhaps the missionary would come here if we asked him. We would pay him well," suggested grandpa.

"If something can be done for him, do you think that the missionary would come here, Kado?"

"I will go and see. He often goes to the homes when it is not possible to take patients to the hospital. I will hurry back," said Kado, going to the door. Addu called him back. "Please do not go, Kado. It will not do any good. It is too late. Already the poison from my arm has gone into my body. I can feel the pain and the fever. It is no use now, Kado. I will die."

Kado knelt down beside Addu's bed on the floor, and said, earnestly, "Just have faith, Addu. Remember how the missionary told us about the God in heaven, and how He healed many people, even some that were already dead. The God in heaven loves you, Addu. Remember the Jesus song? 'Yes, I love Jesus, for He died for me.' Try to believe that He can help you now."

But little Addu did not hear Kado's plea. He had passed into unconsciousness because of the fever. Kado turned to Addu's mother. "You believe that the God in heaven can help Addu, don't you?"

Addu's mother was crying softly, but she nodded her head.

"I will go now and bring the missionary back with me," said the youth.

Kado ran down the path toward the mission, and, as he ran, he prayed. He had faith to believe that the missionary could help Addu with the power of the God in heaven. He was quite out of breath when he reached the mission hospital. The missionary doctor was busy, but he paused to hear Kado's short sentences.

"It's Addu. His arm is broken. He's been very sick for eight days. He is burning with fever, and has terrible pains in his body. He is sure he is going to die."

"Did his mother send for me, Kado?" asked the missionary.

Kado nodded.

"What has been done for him, Kado? The usual cowmanure treatment, no doubt, and other medicines prescribed by the charm doctor."

Again Kado nodded assent. The mission lady came in at that moment, and the doctor explained to her In a few words what had happened.

"Why, oh, why, do they wait so long before calling us?" she said. "They try all the methods of the charm doctor. When they are convinced that these will not help, they come to us as a last resort—and often it is too late."

"From what Kado has just told me," said the missionary sadly, "I fear it is too late in this case. He is a frail little fellow, and he does not have much to fight with. I have missed him from the evening meetings. He has shown quite an interest lately. I must go and see what can be done for him. Are you ready, Kado?"

"I will go with you, too," said the mission lady. "I have the kit ready: iodine, swabs, bandages, the magic needle—everything. Will you need an anesthetic or sedatives?"

"Bring along that other black kit. We will see."

Calling his faithful native helpers, Tim and Orlo, the doctor said, "Bring the stretcher. There may be a small chance that we can help him by bringing him to the hospital. Let's hurry."

The group followed Kado down the trail and across the field. The missionary doctor was thoughtful and serious. The missionary lady, too, looked grave as she followed close behind him. Bringing up the rear were Tim and Orlo with the stretcher. When they neared the humble home, Addu's mother came down the path to meet them.

"I fear it is too late," she sobbed. "My little Addu will die. He does not speak to me any more; his body is so hot with fever. Oh, if you had only come sooner."

"I would have if you had called me," said the missionary gently. "You see, I do not come unless I am called. We will look at the boy, however, and see if there is still a chance. We must be of good cheer and have faith and trust in the God in heaven, for without His help we can do nothing. He alone is the One who can help your little Addu, if it is His will."

The missionary doctor followed the mother into the house. The old grandmother, who had been muttering weird incantations over the sick boy, now moved over to a far comer of the room, still moving her lips and wringing her hands. Grandpa stood anxiously by the door, watching every move of the missionary as he made a brief examination of the boy on the mat on the floor.

Slowly the missionary arose from his knees and spoke to his wife in low tones: "Compound fracture; very weak and undernourished; lungs filled up. We cannot give an anesthetic, but that arm must be amputated at once."

Then he explained to the mother what would have to be done in order to save the boy's life. The grandmother came from the corner of the room and said, "Let him die. They shall not cut it."

The situation seemed hopeless. Although the mother at times seemed willing, the grandmother was firm. Bound by many years of superstition, she insisted that to cut off the arm would bring a curse on the whole family. It would be better that the boy die.

"Haven't we had troubles enough without any more?" she screamed in her high-pitched voice. "The spirits are already angry; their curse is already upon us!"

"But the God in heaven can break that curse," said the missionary kindly. "Would it not be only fair to give Him a chance to show His power? Little Addu has a chance, if you are willing to try."

The grandmother was almost frantic as she shouted at the missionary doctor, "The spirits are already angry; their curse is already upon us!"

Finally, after much tactful and gentle persuasion on the part of the missionary and the mission lady, the mother said, "Yes, yes, please do what you can to help him. I trust him to you, I do not want my little Addu to die."

The old grandmother went back to her comer, still muttering and wringing her hands. Grandpa took up his stick and went hobbling outside. He sat in the shade of a tree where he would be out of the way.

The doctor called Tim and Orlo, who gently lifted the unconscious Addu on to the stretcher. Then the little procession, which now included Addu's mother, started slowly back to the mission hospital with their precious burden. As they were crossing the field, Addu stirred. He opened his eyes and called, "Kado, please sing for me before I die. Sing the Jesus song."

Kado walked beside the stretcher. He took Addu's good hand in his, and began to sing the song the little boy loved. It was hard for Kado to sing, knowing that his little friend was so seriously ill; but he would sing to give the sick boy courage. Choking back the sobs that seemed to come up in his throat, Kado sang again and again, until they reached the door of the mission hospital. Perhaps Addu had not heard the song at all, Kado thought, as he started to release his hold on the brown hand that he held. But Addu tightened his fingers around Kado's for a moment and said feebly, "Thank you, Kado, for the Jesus song."

Tenderly Tim and Orlo lifted the boy on to the hospital bed, put away the stretcher, and stood waiting to take further orders from the missionary doctor. The mission lady bathed the little body with a disinfectant, while the missionary doctor prepared the necessary equipment for the operation.

Kado stood by the weeping mother, and although he did not say a word, his presence seemed to be a comfort to her.

When everything was ready, the missionary doctor called the group together for prayer. It was a new experience for the mother, but she listened to the earnest words spoken in reverence to the God in heaven. The doctor asked for guidance in doing all that was humanly possible for the eight-year-old boy. Then he prayed for the mother, that she, too, might learn to lean upon the God in heaven. The missionary doctor arose from his knees and, with trust and confidence, went to work. Close by his side stood the mission lady, assisting him with swabs and bandages. When it was all over, the doctor took off his white coat, and the mission lady put the instruments in the container to be sterilized. The doctor wiped the perspiration from his forehead and said, "I have done the best I could. We must now leave the rest to the Great Physician."

Long after the three boys, Tim, Orlo, and Kado, had gone to bed, lights were burning in the mission hospital. The missionary doctor, his wife, and the mother of Addu, sat watching the sleeping boy. His face was still feverish, but he was resting better than he had for several days.

"Is my little Addu better?" asked the mother anxiously. "Tell me, will he not die?"

"We cannot tell," said the doctor, "for he still has a battle to fight: pneumonia and rheumatic fever. But if it is the will of the heavenly Father, your little Addu will soon show signs of a change for the better. We have prayed; now we must trust."

The mother stayed at the bedside of her son the rest of the night. In the morning as the sun arose over the redtiled roofs of the mission, Addu opened his eyes, and said, "Mother, I feel better. The pain is gone. I think I will get well. I do not want to die. I want to be a missionary doctor. I want to tell the people about the God in heaven who makes people well. I want to be a Christian like Kado. I, too, want to sing the Jesus song."

Then the mother went back across the fields to her home. The grandmother met her at the door. She, too, seemed happy at the news that Addu would live. "He must stay at the hospital until the fever is gone and his arm is healed," said the mother.

The grandmother had been thinking it all over during the long night. She, too, was beginning to have confidence in the missionary doctor. Perhaps he was right after all, she thought.

KADO BRINGS THE MEDICINE

IN THE little village where Kado lived, many people had a terrible fever, and the mission hospital was full of patients. The missionary and his helpers did all they could to help the sick. Every available space was put to use, and Tim and Orlo were busy bringing in more patients who needed help. The mission lady and the native nurses were working hard to relieve the suffering. Soon the supplies of much-needed medicine became low.

"I will have to go to the nearest hospital to get more," said the missionary one morning.

"But it will take two days by oxcart," said Kado, knowing that precious time would be lost. "Let me go up across the hills. I know a shorter way. It is not far from the village where I used to live. After you cross the bridge over the creek you take the road to the left."

"But, Kado," objected the missionary kindly, "that is a long and dangerous journey by foot through the hills. I would not consider letting you make the trip alone. If only Tim or Orlo knew the way. Perhaps one of them could go with you."

"They are needed here," said Kado. "I am sure I can make it all right. If I go this morning, I can be back by dark if I hurry."

Preparations were made quickly for Kado to go. The mission lady prepared a lunch for the trip. Before he left, the three bowed for a moment of prayer.

"I am not afraid," said Kado. "I am not going for myself; it is for those who are sick and need the medicine. God will go with me, and bring me back safely for their sakes. I will go now."

Away went Kado, his face shining in the glow of the morning sun. With a song on his lips and a prayer in his heart he hurried along the path and across the bridge. He knew the way; he had traveled it before when he first came to the mission school.

By noon he reached the village and secured the packet of precious medicine. He retraced his steps toward his own village with the medicine tucked safely in the folds of his wrap-around garment. It began to grow dark late in the afternoon as heavy clouds hid the sun from view. The village was still some distance away, but Kado knew the path.

It had been a long day for Kado. He had been walking rapidly ever since morning. The muscles of his body were beginning to show signs of weariness, but he hurried on. There was no time to lose, for the medicine was needed at the hospital.

The clouds grew darker, and it looked as though it might rain soon. Kado hoped he would be able to reach the village before the storm broke, because he must not let that precious package of medicine get wet.

Soon the rain began to come down, and big drops splashed on Kado's arms and face. His wrap-around garment began to feel rather damp as the rain continued.

"If I can only get to that bridge," thought Kado, running as fast as his tired feet would go. The planks of the bridge made a rumbling sound as Kado ran across them. Then, instead of going on in the pouring rain,

Kado slid down the bank of the creek, and crawled under the bridge.

It provided a crude shelter from the rain. Kado felt the package and found it dry.

"I will stay under here until it stops raining." Kado was glad for a chance to rest. He had been hurrying so fast he was very tired. He sat on a large flat rock and listened to the sound of the rain on the bridge. He was thankful for the shelter. As Kado sat waiting on the big rock under the bridge, it became quite dark.

"I hope it does not rain like this all night," said Kado. "I would have been at the hospital by this time, if it hadn't started to rain."

Darker and darker it grew, and the rain kept falling. To keep from growing sleepy, Kado began to sing. His favorite song, of course, was the Jesus song, and he sang it over and over. He became sleepy in spite of his efforts to stay awake, and stretched himself out on the rock. He held his precious bundle close within the folds of his garment. He said a good-night prayer and was soon fast asleep.

How long Kado slept on the rock under the bridge, he did not know. When he awoke it was still raining. Suddenly he was aware of something beside him on the rock, and he sensed danger. "The medicine!" Kado prayed. "I must take it to the hospital for the sick people. Please keep me from harm so I can take it to them safely."

Kado lay perfectly still, knowing that if he were to run from whatever animal it might be it would soon overtake him. He could hear a sniffing sound close beside him. He could feel cold nostrils on his bare arm and shoulder as the animal smelled him. A heavy paw was placed on the boy's hip as the intruder continued to investigate. Kado was almost paralyzed with fright, but he dared not move a muscle. Suddenly the animal began to purr. A warm, wet tongue licked Kado's bare arm and shoulder. Kado's heart beat fast and he continued to pray. The warm, wet tongue licked his hair and around his neck and ear. Then suddenly the big animal lay down beside Kado, and with that same wet tongue began to wash the rain from his own fur coat. The purring continued and blended with the sound of falling rain. The two sounds might have been a soothing lullaby for some, but not to Kado. His eyes were wide open, staring into the inky darkness. Whatever the animal was, it wanted shelter from the rain, and now it was sound asleep on the rock beside him.

When it began to grow light in the east, Kado felt the big animal stir. It opened its mouth and yawned; then it stretched and walked away. As the animal scrambled up the creek bank, Kado took courage and sat up to look. A half-grown spotted leopard had slept beside him during the night!

Soon Kado also scrambled out from under the bridge and started toward the village. Only a few drops of rain dripped from the trees above him. He held his precious package safely in the folds of his garment and hurried on. He breathed a prayer of thankfulness to the Lord who watches over His trusting children.

The precious package was delivered safe and dry into the hands of the missionary doctor. Kado was given a good breakfast at the mission house, and, while he ate, he recounted his adventure of the night to the mission lady. She listened carefully as he told of the leopard that purred and licked his neck and shoulder. Then the woman said reverently, "'The angel of the Lord encampeth round about them that fear Him, and delivereth them.'"

Kado was given a generous reward in cash for his faithful work in bringing the medicine to the hospital; but money was not the only reward he received. In his heart he was happy, knowing that he had helped the people in his village who were in need.

Kado had jewels for Jesus, his Friend. They were the boys and girls to whom he had told the story of Jesus and how He would soon return.

KADO'S JEWELS

KADO and his three brothers, Tari, Lesso, and Con, were spending a quiet afternoon under the shade trees near the mission house. The three boys had been listening as Kado read some of the beautiful stories from the Bible the mission lady had given him. When the story of buried treasure was concluded, Tari said, "I wish I could dig in our rice fields and find a box of buried treasure. Think of the many things we could buy with a lot of money."

"Suppose," began Con, "that a rich queen hid a lot of jewels in a cave behind our house and we found them!"

"What would you do with a queen's jewels?" asked Lesso with a broad smile.

"Sell them and give the money to the mission," said Con. "I am sure there are many things they could use."

Kado closed his book, laid it in the grass beside him, and said, "Perhaps there is a different meaning in the story of jewels and buried treasure. Do you remember the mission lady telling us there are many precious souls right here in the village who, if we could find them, would be jewels in the King's crown?"

"Oh, yes," said Tari, "I remember. We sang that song, 'When He cometh to make up His jewels.' I know what you mean; but how can we find those jewels?"

"Every day," said Kado, "we can let our light shine. Every day we can speak to someone about how kind and good Jesus is, and how He watches over us and keeps us. If we lead one person to Jesus, that person will tell someone else. Isn't it about time for the meeting to begin? I want to be there for the first song. Let's go."

The four boys scrambled to their feet, and Kado led the way, with his precious Bible under his arm.

There were a number of eager boys and girls already in their places near the mission home. The meeting was held under the trees because the weather was warm. The mission lady had a place for her drawing board and picture roll.

"Kado," said the mission lady, "you are one of the older boys. Would you like to tell the story today? I am sure you have it well in mind."

After a few songs and a prayer, the mission lady announced that Kado would tell the story. The youth's heart was beating rapidly as he stood beside the mission lady and looked into the eager, waiting faces. They were anxious for him to begin the story. These brown boys and girls were jewels, precious jewels for Jesus.

Kado told his story simply, earnestly. His brothers were proud of him as he repeated the story of the hidden treasure in the field, which he had read from the Bible only a short time before.

The mission lady thought of many people who had been brought to the mission by Kado. There were many others who had been helped by watching Kado's honest face and by hearing him sing the Jesus song as he worked. Even the mission lady, in moments of discouragement, took heart when she thought of Kado.

In the glad day when Jesus comes to make up His jewels, He will find many souls for His kingdom because of boys and girls like Kado.